home-grown
harvest

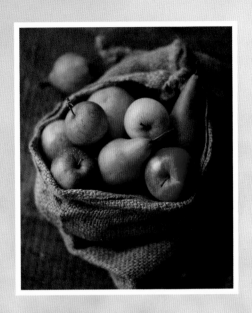

home-grown
harvest

delicious ways to enjoy your
seasonal fruit and vegetables

RYLAND
PETERS
& SMALL
LONDON NEW YORK

Senior Designer Iona Hoyle

Editor Rebecca Woods

Picture Research Emily Westlake

Head of production Patricia Harrington

Art Director Leslie Harrington

Publishing Director Alison Starling

Indexer Sandra Shotter

First published in 2011
by Ryland Peters & Small, Inc.
519 Broadway, 5th Floor
New York, NY 10012

www.rylandpeters.com

10 9 8 7 6 5 4 3 2 1

Printed in China

Text © Ghillie Başan, Fiona Beckett, Celia Brooks
Brown, Maxine Clark, Ross Dobson, Tonia George,
Brian Glover, Amanda Grant, Annie Nichols, Jane
Noraika, Louise Pickford, Isidora Popovic, Sarah
Randell, Annie Rigg, Jennie Shapter, Fiona Smith,
Sonia Stevenson, Linda Tubby, Sunil Vijayakar,
Fran Warde, Laura Washburn, Lindy Wildsmith
and Ryland Peters & Small 2011

Design and commissioned photographs
© Ryland Peters & Small 2011

ISBN 978 1 84975 149 0

Library of Congress Cataloging-in-Publication Data

Home-grown harvest : delicious ways to enjoy your
seasonal fruit and vegetables.
       p. cm.
   Includes index.
   ISBN 978-1-84975-149-0
   1. Cooking (Fruit) 2. Cooking (Vegetables) 3.
Cookbooks. I. Ryland Peters & Small.
   TX811.H66 2011
   641.6'4--dc23
                                          2011029183

Notes

• All spoon measurements are level
unless otherwise specified.

• Eggs are medium unless otherwise specified.
Uncooked or partly cooked eggs should not be
served to the very young, the very old, those with
compromised immune systems, or to pregnant
women.

• When a recipe calls for the grated peel of a citrus
fruit, buy unwaxed fruit and wash well before using.
If you can only find treated fruit, scrub well in warm
soapy water before using.

• Weights and measurements have been rounded
up or down slightly to make measuring easier.

• Ovens should be preheated to the specified
temperature. If using a fan-assisted oven, cooking
times should be reduced according to the
manufacturer's instructions.

• To sterilize preserving jars, wash them in hot,
soapy water and rinse in boiling water. Place in
a large saucepan and cover with hot water. With
the saucepan lid on, bring the water to a boil and
continue boiling for 15 minutes. Turn off the heat
and leave the jars in the hot water until just before
they are to be filled. Invert the jars onto a clean
dish towel to dry. Sterilize the lids for 5 minutes,
by boiling or according to the manufacturer's
instructions. Jars should be filled and sealed while
they are still hot.

contents

introduction

Growing your own fruit and vegetables is immensely satisfying—and is quickly becoming fashionable again. Food-loving gardeners are once more beginning to incorporate edible varieties of plants, as well as beautiful ornamental ones, into gardens that resemble the more functional spaces of our childhoods. Even in inner cities, where space is at a premium, many urbanites are finding that allotting precious space on a roof terrace or small patio for a few tomato or strawberry pots not only brings the benefit of the produce itself, but also provides a pastoral escape from a stressful lifestyle. And for those who struggle horticulturally, there is healthy growth in farmers' markets, especially within cities, providing local venues to buy the freshest produce direct from source and talk to the growers themselves about the best ways to prepare those sweet young carrots or deliciously earthy new potatoes.

This rise in popularity of home- or locally-grown fresh produce marks a deeply positive change in attitudes towards food, and is indicative of a quiet but growing backlash against a global, profit-driven food trade that lacks respect for the environment and the seasons and delivers disappointing produce. Food that travels long distances can be tasteless—harvested long before it is ready and shipped in refrigerated transport that stops ripening in it's tracks. Tomatoes bought in winter can be tough, floury, and bland, nothing like the deep-red, sweet-smelling tomatoes that are picked off the vine in the height of summer. Additionally, many of the nutrients present when produce is first picked are lost during the long journey between the field and the plate.

In contrast, home-grown produce is cultivated with care for the environment—and you can taste the difference. There is great pleasure to be gained from eating what is seasonally available—paying greater respect to the natural order of the seasons yields wonderful results in the finished dish. Not only this, but putting in time in the garden can also lead to a healthy reduction in supermarket expenditure

But to say this to you, the holder of this book, is likely to be preaching to the converted. Your back yard, vegetable patch, or even window box may already be abundant with fresh fruit and vegetables, but the dilemma is what now to do with this produce that you have spent time and care nurturing? One of the downsides of growing your own can be the sense of dé jà vu that haunts meal times. Dinners can seem suspiciously similar when all created from the same crop, and finding new inspiration can be tricky. For the home-grower it becomes customary for each visiting friend or relative to leave the house with a goodie bag laden with fresh fruit or vegetables that have become tiresome or that there is simply no chance of consuming before they spoil.

This is where **Home-grown Harvest** can help. Providing recipes for all your favorite fruit and vegetables, it ensures that there are numerous options for using each so that you don't have to cook the same dish time and time again in order to use up your produce. And because most seasonal locally-grown vegetables can be picked at their very best, many of the recipes are rustic and unfussy and truly let the flavor of the produce speak for itself.

The book is arranged as an easy reference guide with the recipes for each vegetable or fruit grouped together. Although, as much of the produce may be featured not only in it's own chapter but also in combinations with other fruit or vegetables, don't forget to check the index for other recipes, too. And be sure to take note of the handy tips, which offer further advice on preparing, storing, and truly savoring the rewards of your labor.

root vegetables

mashed potato pie with bacon, leeks, & cheese
potato & parsnip croquettes ❧ indian potato curry with
toor dhal ❧ potato tortilla with red pepper tapenade
roasted new potatoes ❧ bay-roasted hasselbacks
potatoes dauphinoise ❧ hash browns
sweet potato & coconut soup with thai pesto
sesame sweet potato with peanut dipping sauce
roasted sweet potato & macadamia nut salad
tagine of sweet potato, shallots, & carrots
roast sweet potato & chicken pie ❧ spiced carrot soup
roasted carrots with barley risotto ❧ madeira-glazed
roast carrots ❧ spiced carrot dip ❧ carrots with
cream & herbs ❧ vichy carrots with fresh ginger
carrot & walnut cake with cream cheese filling
parsnip, chorizo, & chestnut soup ❧ parsnip, apple,
& thyme soup ❧ honey-roast parsnip, carrot,
& shallot tart ❧ beet & beef tagine with oranges
cardinal's salad ❧ beet, fennel, & apple chutney
beet & horseradish relish ❧ mini chocolate,
beet, & cherry cakes

If you've got a successful crop of potatoes this year and you need inspiration for how best to use them, this pie is a great option. Bacon, leeks, and cheese make a particularly perfect trio, but you can add just about anything to this versatile dish. You should have potatoes at the very least, and cheese of some sort, and something green for a bit of color —after that, anything goes! The croquettes are particularly good if you grow a floury variety of potato as it fluffs up nicely when boiled and mashed. The parsnip adds an interesting flavor dimension, as it is a little bitter and sweet at the same time.

mashed potato pie with bacon, leeks, & cheese

2¼ lbs. floury potatoes, peeled

2 tablespoons olive oil

1 onion, finely chopped

2 small leeks, thinly sliced

½ cup thick-sliced bacon or pancetta

2 tablespoons butter

1 cup milk or light cream (or a bit of both)

1 egg, beaten

a pinch of paprika

a large handful of fresh parsley leaves, chopped

⅔ cup grated firm cheese, such as Gruyère

sea salt and freshly ground black pepper

a 10-inch round baking dish, well buttered

serves 4–6

Halve or quarter the potatoes depending on their size; they should be about the same to cook evenly. Put them in a large saucepan, add sufficient cold water to cover, salt well, and bring to a boil. Simmer for about 20 minutes, until tender and easily pierced with a skewer.

Meanwhile, heat the oil in a skillet set over low heat. Add the onion and leeks and cook gently for about 10 minutes, until soft. Add the bacon and cook for 3–5 minutes, until just browned. Season with salt and set aside.

Preheat the oven to 375°F.

Drain the potatoes and mash coarsely, mixing in the butter and milk. Season well and add the egg. Stir to combine thoroughly.

Stir in the leek mixture, paprika, parsley, and half the cheese. Transfer to the prepared baking dish and spread evenly. Sprinkle over the remaining cheese and bake in the preheated oven for 35–45 minutes, until well browned. Serve immediately.

potato & parsnip croquettes

1 lb. potatoes, peeled and quartered

1 parsnip, peeled and quartered

3 tablespoons butter

2 tablespoons finely chopped fresh parsley

2 eggs

1 cup dry breadcrumbs from a day-old loaf of bread

2 tablespoons all-purpose flour, for dusting

vegetable oil, for shallow-frying

sea salt and freshly ground black pepper

sweet German mustard, to serve

makes 18 croquettes

Put the potatoes and parsnip in a large saucepan and cover with boiling water. Set over high heat and boil for 12–15 minutes until tender. Drain and return to the warm pan. Add the 2 tablespoons of the butter and mash well until the mixture is lump-free. Stir in the parsley and season well with salt and pepper. Cover and refrigerate until the mixture is completely chilled.

Break the eggs into a bowl and beat well to combine. Put the breadcrumbs in a separate bowl. Lightly flour your hands and a work surface. Take 1 heaped tablespoon of the potato mixture and form it into a small sausage, tapping the ends on the work surface so that they are flattened rather than tapered. Dip the croquette in the beaten egg, then roll it in the crumbs until coated. Put on a baking sheet lined with baking parchment. Repeat until all of the potato mixture has been used and refrigerate until ready to cook.

Put the 1 tablespoon butter in a skillet and pour in sufficient oil to come halfway up the sides of the pan. Heat the skillet over medium heat until the butter begins to sizzle. To test if the oil is hot enough, sprinkle a few crumbs into it—they should sizzle on contact. Cook the croquettes in batches for 2–3 minutes, turning often, until golden and crisp all over. Remove from the oil using a slotted spoon and drain on paper towels to remove excess oil. Serve warm with the mustard on the side. **Pictured on page 50.**

The humble potato is fantastic for absorbing the rich flavors of fragrant spices, such as in this curry, which makes a hearty meal with the addition of lentils, too. The tortilla may not look that substantial, but thanks to the creamy Taleggio cheese, it packs a super-rich taste punch and is more than enough for four to enjoy as a starter or snack.

potato tortilla with red pepper tapenade

10–12 small, new boiling potatoes, thickly sliced

1 small red onion, roughly chopped

1 tablespoon olive oil

1 cup vegetable stock

a handful of fresh flat leaf parsley, chopped

4 oz. Taleggio cheese, chopped or torn into large chunks

2 eggs, lightly beaten

red pepper tapenade

1 large red bell pepper

1 garlic clove, chopped

⅓ cup pine nuts, lightly toasted

2 tablespoons olive oil

½ cup finely grated Parmesan cheese

serves 4

To make the tapenade, preheat the oven to 425ºF. Put a baking sheet in the oven for a few minutes to heat. Put the red bell pepper on the sheet and cook it in the preheated oven for about 15 minutes, turning often until the skin is starting to blacken and puff up. Transfer it to a clean plastic bag, seal, and let cool. When the bell pepper is cool enough to handle, peel off the skin, discard the seeds, roughly tear or chop the flesh, and put it in a food processor. Add the garlic, pine nuts, and oil and process until smooth. Spoon into a bowl, add the Parmesan, and stir well to combine.

Put the potatoes, onion, and olive oil in a skillet set over high heat and cook for 1 minute. Add the stock and cook for about 10 minutes, until the stock has evaporated and the vegetables start to sizzle in the skillet. Stir through the parsley and put the pieces of cheese among the potatoes. Pour the eggs into the skillet and cook for 2–3 minutes until they start to puff up around the edges. Give the skillet a couple of firm shakes—this will make it easier to get the cooked tortilla out. Meanwhile, preheat the broiler to high. Put the skillet under the hot broiler and cook the tortilla for 1–2 minutes, until the top is golden but still wobbly in the centre. Use a spatula to smear some of the tapenade onto the base of a serving plate and carefully slide the tortilla onto the plate. Cut into 4 slices and eat direct from the plate with extra tapenade on the side.

indian potato curry with toor dhal

1¼ cups yellow lentils

3 tablespoons vegetable oil

½ teaspoon mustard seeds

½ teaspoon fenugreek seeds

1 teaspoon grated fresh ginger

1 teaspoon crushed garlic

1 teaspoon chili powder

1½ teaspoons ground coriander

½ teaspoon ground turmeric

4 tomatoes, skinned and chopped

1 teaspoon salt

1½ lbs. floury potatoes, cut into 1-inch chunks

sea salt and freshly ground black pepper

to serve

2 tablespoons freshly chopped cilantro, plus extra sprigs

½ teaspoon garam masala

basmati rice

serves 4

Wash the lentils well in several changes of water. Heat the oil in a large saucepan over low heat. Add the mustard and fenugreek seeds. When they begin to pop, stir in the ginger and garlic and fry for 30 seconds.

Add the chili powder, ground coriander, and turmeric, and stir-fry for a further 30 seconds. Add the tomatoes and lentils, cover with 2½ cups water, add the salt, then bring to a boil. Reduce the heat, cover and simmer for 20–30 minutes or until the lentils are just soft.

Add the potatoes and simmer over low heat for 10–15 minutes or until the potatoes are tender. Season with salt and pepper.

Serve sprinkled with chopped cilantro, garam masala, and sprigs of fresh cilantro. Basmati rice makes a suitable accompaniment.

roasted new potatoes

2 lbs. small poatoes, unpeeled and scrubbed

3 tablespoons olive oil

2 garlic cloves, whole and unpeeled

a few sprigs of fresh rosemary

serves 4

Preheat the oven to 375°F.

Cut any big potatoes in half so that they are all roughly the same size. Put them into a large, heavy-based roasting pan. Drizzle a little olive oil over the top. Add the garlic and sprigs of rosemary.

Put the pan into the oven and roast for 20 minutes. Take the pan out of the oven and move the potatoes around with a wooden spoon. Roast a little longer if they are still not ready.

bay-roasted hasselbacks

24 small poatoes, unpeeled and scrubbed

approximately 20 fresh bay leaves, torn in half lengthwise

1 tablespoon unsalted butter

3 tablespoons olive oil

1–2 garlic cloves, crushed

sea salt flakes and freshly ground black pepper

serves 4–6

Preheat the oven to 375°F.

To prepare the potatoes, spear each potato lengthwise with a skewer about ¼ inch from the base, slice widthwise across the potato as far as the skewer, then remove the skewer.

Insert a couple of pieces of bay leaf, in each sliced potato. Melt the butter with the oil in a heavy-based roasting pan over moderate heat. Stir in the garlic and gently add the potatoes in a single layer. Move them around for 2–3 minutes to color slightly, then season with sea salt flakes and black pepper.

Roast the potatoes in the preheated oven for 25–30 minutes until golden brown and tender. As they cook, the potatoes will open out like a fan.

potatoes dauphinoise

2 lbs. waxy potatoes, thinly sliced

1¼ cups freshly grated Parmesan cheese

freshly grated nutmeg

1¼ cups heavy cream

sea salt and freshly ground black pepper

a shallow, ovenproof dish, buttered

serves 6

Preheat the oven to 325°F.

Layer the potatoes in the dish, seasoning each layer with cheese, nutmeg, salt, and pepper. Pour over the cream and sprinkle any remaining cheese over the top. Bake in the preheated oven for about 1 hour or until the potatoes are tender and the top is golden and crisp.

hash browns

2 tablespoons butter

1 onion, chopped

1½ lbs. large potatoes, peeled and grated

1 egg white, beaten

vegetable oil, for deep frying

sea salt and freshly ground black pepper

makes 16

Heat the butter in a skillet, then add the onion, cover with a lid, and cook over low heat until soft.

Put the potatoes into a large mixing bowl and stir in the softened onions. Stir in the egg white and season generously.

Fill a large saucepan one-third full with vegetable oil. Heat to 375°F (or until a blob of the potato mixture browns within a few seconds).

Roll the potato mixture into walnut-sized balls, then flatten slightly before adding to the hot oil. Fry in batches for 2–3 minutes, until golden brown. Drain on paper towels and serve with extra salt, for sprinkling.

Sweet potatoes make an excellent ingredient for soups. When blended they take on a velvety, creamy texture. Here, their sweetness is cut through with some full-on and spicy Asian flavors in the form of a Thai-style pesto, which really brings this soup to life.

sweet potato & coconut soup with thai pesto

1 tablespoon light olive oil

1 lb. sweet potato, peeled and chopped into chunks

1 red onion, chopped

1 tablespoon Thai red curry paste

2 cups vegetable stock

2 cups coconut milk

thai pesto

⅔ cup unsalted peanuts, lightly toasted

2 garlic cloves, chopped

2 teaspoons finely grated fresh ginger

2 large green chiles, seeded and chopped

a small bunch of fresh cilantro

a large handful of fresh mint leaves

a large handful of fresh basil leaves

2 tablespoons light soy sauce or Thai fish sauce

2 tablespoons freshly squeezed lime juice

1 tablespoon soft light brown sugar

serves 4

Put the oil in a heavy-based saucepan set over medium heat. Add the sweet potato and onion, partially cover with a lid, and cook for 15 minutes, stirring often, until they are soft and just starting to turn golden. Increase the heat to high, add the curry paste, and stir-fry with the sweet potato for 3–4 minutes so that the pasta cooks and becomes fragrant. Add the stock and coconut milk and bring to the boil. Transfer the mixture to a food processor or blender and whizz until smooth. Return the soup to a clean saucepan.

To make the pesto, put all of the ingredients in a food processor or blender and whizz, occasionally scraping down the sides of the bowl, until you have a chunky green paste and the ingredients are all evenly chopped. Gently reheat the soup, then ladle into warmed serving bowls. Top with a generous spoonful of Thai pesto to serve.

✳ tip

Sweet potatoes are very versatile and can be substituted in place of white potatoes in most recipes, especially the paler varieties. Store them in a cool, dark, dry place, but they should never be refrigerated, as this causes their centres to harden and their flavor to be impaired.

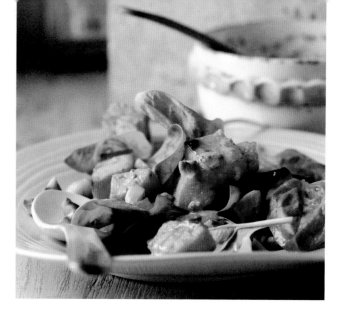

Sweet potato is wonderful paired with nuts, and these two light bites make the most of that heavenly combination. Golden sesame wedges are served with a peanut dipping sauce for a moreish snack, while macadamia nuts add a great crunch to this roasted sweet potato salad.

sesame sweet potato with peanut dipping sauce

1½ lbs. sweet potatoes, well scrubbed but unpeeled, cut lengthwise into thick wedges

2 tablespoons olive oil

1 tablespoon sesame oil

1 tablespoon sesame seeds

sea salt

fresh cilantro, coarsely torn or chopped, to serve

dipping sauce

2 tablespoons organic peanut butter

1 tablespoon freshly squeezed lime juice

½ red chile, seeded and sliced

1 tablespoon soy sauce

1 tablespoon tomato ketchup

sea salt and freshly ground black pepper

serves 6–8

Arrange the sweet potato wedges in a single layer on a baking sheet, then sprinkle with the olive and sesame oils, sesame seeds, and salt. Roast in a preheated oven at 400°F for 35 minutes or until tender (the cooking time will vary depending on the size of the wedges).

Meanwhile, to prepare the dipping sauce, put the peanut butter, lime juice, chile, soy sauce, and tomato ketchup in a food processor, add 4 tablespoons hot water, and blend until smooth. Add salt and pepper to taste, then pour into a saucepan and heat gently.

Sprinkle the wedges with the cilantro and serve with a separate bowl of the dipping sauce.

Variation To simplify this recipe even further, serve the wedges with store-bought sweet chile sauce.

roasted sweet potato & macadamia nut salad

3 sweet potatoes (about 10 oz. each), peeled

1 tablespoon olive oil

1 teaspoon sea salt flakes

2½ oz. raw macadamia nuts, roughly chopped

7 oz. baby spinach leaves, washed

dressing

2 tablespoons macadamia or olive oil

1 tablespoon cider vinegar

1 teaspoon wholegrain mustard

sea salt and freshly ground black pepper

serves 4

Preheat the oven to 375°F.

Cut the sweet potatoes into 1-inch cubes and toss in a bowl with the olive oil and salt flakes. Tip onto a baking sheet and roast in the preheated oven for 10 minutes.

Put the macadamia nuts in the bowl and toss with any residual oil. Add to the sweet potatoes and roast in the hot oven for 10 minutes, giving the sweet potatoes 20 minutes in total.

To make the dressing, mix together the macadamia oil, vinegar, and mustard in a small bowl. Season to taste with salt and pepper.

Arrange the spinach leaves on a serving platter and top with the sweet potatoes and macadamia nuts. Drizzle or spoon the dressing over the top and serve immediately.

tagine of sweet potato, shallots, & carrots

2–3 tablespoons olive oil plus a pat of butter

1½-inch piece fresh ginger, peeled and finely chopped or grated

1–2 cinnamon sticks or 1–2 teaspoons ground cinnamon

16 small shallots, peeled and left whole

1¾ lbs. sweet potato, peeled and cut into bite-sized pieces

2 medium carrots, peeled and cut into bite-sized pieces

¾ cup ready-to-eat pitted prunes

1 tablespoon dark, runny honey

1¾ cups vegetable or chicken stock

leaves from a small bunch of fresh cilantro, roughly chopped

a few fresh mint leaves, chopped

sea salt and freshly ground black pepper

couscous, to serve (optional)

serves 4–6

Heat the olive oil and butter in a tagine or heavy-based casserole. Add the ginger and cinnamon sticks. Toss in the shallots and when they begin to color add the sweet potato and the carrots. Sauté for 2–3 minutes, stirring, then add the prunes and the honey. Pour in the stock and bring it to a boil. Reduce the heat, cover, and cook gently for about 25 minutes.

Uncover and stir in some of the cilantro and mint. Season to taste and reduce the liquid, if necessary, by cooking for a further 2–3 minutes uncovered. The vegetables should be tender and slightly caramelized in a very syrupy sauce. Sprinkle with the remaining cilantro and mint and serve immediately with couscous, if liked.

Two hearty, warming dishes: this syrupy, caramelized tagine can be adapted to what you have grown—try it with butternut squash or pumpkin instead of sweet potato, if you prefer. The sweet potato and chicken pie is a great way to recycle leftover roast chicken, as well as use up vegetable gluts. To obtain the stale bread, use the end pieces from sliced loaves and toast them in the oven, alongside the sweet potatoes.

roast sweet potato & chicken pie

3½ lbs. sweet potatoes, peeled and cut into chunks

3–4 tablespoons olive oil

3 tablespoons butter

1 onion, cubed

4 oz. bacon, chopped

2 celery ribs, chopped

2 cups chopped mushrooms

2 garlic cloves, crushed

2 teaspoons dried thyme

2½–3½ oz. sausages, cooked and chopped

¾ cup chopped vacuum-packed peeled chestnuts

a large handful of fresh parsley leaves, chopped

½ a chicken (about 1½ lbs.), cooked and meat shredded

4 oz. stale or toasted bread, broken into small pieces

5 tablespoons milk

¾ cup chicken stock or water

sea salt and freshly ground black pepper

a 10–12-inch round baking dish, well buttered

serves 4–6

Preheat the oven to 425°F.

Toss the sweet potatoes with the 2 tablespoons of the olive oil and arrange in a single layer on a baking sheet. Roast in the preheated oven for about 45 minutes, until tender and browned. Reduce the oven temperature to 400°F. Let the sweet potatoes cool, then mash with butter to taste and season with salt. Set aside.

Heat the rest of the olive oil in a skillet. Add the onion and cook for 2–3 minutes, until soft. Season with salt, then add the bacon, celery, and mushrooms and cook for 3–5 minutes, stirring often. Add the garlic, thyme, sausage, and chestnuts and cook for about 1 minute. Stir in the parsley and chicken and set aside.

In a bowl, combine the bread pieces and milk and toss to coat. The bread should be moist, you may need to add more milk. Add the bread to the chicken mixture, along with the stock. Stir well. Taste and adjust the seasoning.

Spread the chicken mixture in an even layer in the prepared baking dish. It will dry out slightly with baking, so if it seems dry at the outset, add a bit more of any liquid: stock, milk, or water. Top with the mashed sweet potato, spread evenly. Bake in the preheated oven for about 45 minutes. (The sweet potato won't brown but should start to blacken slightly where peaked.)

The delicate flavor of carrots is best blended with vegetable stock or water as chicken muddies the flavor of really good carrots. However, if you're doubtful of your carrots' flavor, go for a good chicken stock.

spiced carrot soup

3 tablespoons butter

1 onion, chopped

1¾ lbs. carrots, chopped

2 teaspoons ground coriander

½ teaspoon ground ginger

¼ teaspoon chili powder

4 cups vegetable stock or water

4 tablespoons heavy cream

2 tablespoons safflower oil

2-inch piece fresh ginger, cut into matchsticks

sea salt and freshly ground black pepper

serves 4

Melt the butter in a large saucepan and sauté the onion for about 5–8 minutes, until softened. Add the carrots, coriander, ground ginger, and chili powder and stir into the butter to coat them and release the flavor of the spices. Season well, then pour in the stock. Simmer for 40 minutes.

Transfer the contents of the pan to a blender in batches (or use a handheld blender) and liquidize to a smooth purée. Stir in the cream. Add a little more water if it is too thick and season to taste.

Heat the safflower oil in a skillet over high heat and fry the ginger for 1 minute, or until crisp.

Divide the soup equally between 4 bowls, garnish with the fried ginger and serve.

roasted carrots with barley risotto

2 tablespoons light olive oil

12 baby carrots, ends trimmed

2 tablespoons butter

2 sprigs of fresh thyme

2 garlic cloves, unpeeled and cut in half

2 cups chicken stock

1 tablespoon light soy sauce

1¼ cups pearl barley

3 heaped tablespoons finely grated Parmesan cheese

sea salt and freshly ground black pepper

serves 4

Heat the oil in a skillet until very hot. Add the carrots and cook for 8–10 minutes, turning every 2 minutes, until golden. If your skillet isn't big enough you may need to do this in batches. Add ⅔ of the butter, the thyme, and garlic to the pan with ½ cup water and season with sea salt and black pepper. Cover the pan with a tight-fitting lid and cook over medium heat for 15–20 minutes, turning often, until the carrots are tender.

Meanwhile, to make the barley risotto, put the stock and soy sauce in a saucepan with 1 quart water and bring to a boil. Add the barley and cook for 45–50 minutes, stirring often, until the barley is soft but not breaking up. Stir in the remaining butter and Parmesan. Serve the carrots on top of the barley.

Variation The carrots could be served hot on a bed of couscous or left to cool and tossed in a salad with beets, toasted pine nuts, and a soft cheese.

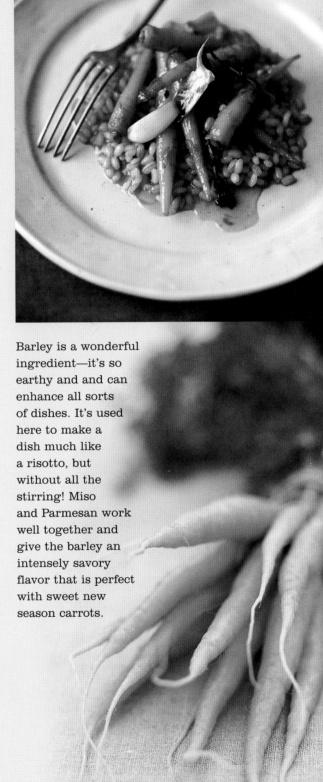

Barley is a wonderful ingredient—it's so earthy and and can enhance all sorts of dishes. It's used here to make a dish much like a risotto, but without all the stirring! Miso and Parmesan work well together and give the barley an intensely savory flavor that is perfect with sweet new season carrots.

carrots **21**

madeira-glazed roast carrots

1½ lbs. young carrots
1 tablespoon olive oil
4 tablespoons unsalted butter
1 teaspoon sugar
½ cup Madeira wine

sea salt and freshly ground black pepper

a handful of fresh flatleaf parsley, corsely chopped, to serve

serves 4–6

Wash and trim the carrots. If large, cut into 1½-inch chunks, but if small or medium, leave them whole. Parboil them in a large saucepan of boiling water for about 10 minutes, leaving them still slightly hard in the middle. Drain.

Meanwhile, heat the oil and butter in a roasting pan in a preheated oven at 400°F until the butter begins to brown. Add the carrots, turn to coat in the oil, then sprinkle with salt, pepper, and the sugar and return to the oven for 10 minutes. Turn them and roast for a further 15 minutes. Add the Madeira and cook until all the liquid has gone. Serve sprinkled with parsley.

spiced carrot dip

1 cup vegetable stock
4 medium carrots, chopped
2 tablespoons light olive oil
1 small red onion, chopped
2 garlic cloves, chopped
1 large red chile, chopped

1 teaspoon fenugreek seeds
1 teaspoon ground cumin
sea salt and white pepper

serves 6–8

Put the stock in a saucepan and add the carrots, oil, onion, and garlic. Bring to a boil, then reduce the heat to low and simmer for 15–20 minutes, until almost all the liquid has evaporated and the carrots are soft. Add the chile, fenugreek seeds, and cumin and stir-fry for 2–3 minutes.

Transfer the mixture to a food processor or blender and whizz until blended but still with a rough texture. Season to taste, transfer to a serving dish, and cover until ready to serve.

carrots with cream & herbs

2 lbs. baby carrots, or medium carrots
3 tablespoons unsalted butter
a sprig of fresh thyme
2 tablespoons crème fraîche or sour cream

several sprigs of fresh chervil, snipped
a small bunch of fresh chives, snipped
fine sea salt

serves 4

Trim the carrots (or if using larger carrots, cut them diagonally into 2-inch slices). Put them in a large saucepan (the carrots should fit in almost a single layer for even cooking). Add the butter and set over low heat. Cook for 3 minutes, until the butter has melted and coated the carrots. Half fill the saucepan with water, then add a pinch of salt and the thyme. Cover and cook for 10–20 minutes, until the water is almost completely evaporated.

Stir in the crème fraîche and add sea salt to taste. Sprinkle the herbs over the top, mix well, and serve.

vichy carrots with fresh ginger

2 lbs. carrots
2 tablespoons finely chopped fresh ginger
4 tablespoons unsalted butter
½ teaspoon sea salt
2 teaspoons sugar

freshly ground black pepper
3 tablespoons freshly chopped cilantro or parsley

serves 8

Cut the carrots into batons or thick rounds and put in a saucepan with the ginger, butter, salt, and sugar. Half-cover with water, bring to a boil, and boil steadily, stirring once or twice, until the water has almost disappeared and the carrots are tender.

Reduce the heat and let the carrots brown a little and caramelize. Season with black pepper and stir in the cilantro or parsley. Serve immediately.

Carrots contain plenty of natural sugars and so are perfect for sweet dishes, such as a classic carrot cake. This version adds walnuts too, and is wonderfully crumbly and soft—and probably best eaten with a spoon! If you are nervous about cutting the cake through the centre, simply spread the creamy frosting over the top of the cooled cake instead.

carrot & walnut cake
with cream cheese filling

2 eggs, separated

½ cup plus 1 tablespoon raw (unrefined) sugar

¾ cup plus 1 tablespoon light olive oil

1 teaspoon baking soda

¾ cup plus 2 tablespoons all-purpose flour

2 teaspoons baking powder

1 teaspoon ground cinnamon

¼ teaspoon freshly grated nutmeg

1 cup grated carrot

⅓ cup walnut halves

cream cheese frosting

8 oz. cream cheese

1 stick butter, cubed

3 tablespoons brown sugar

2–3 tablespoons maple syrup

a 7-inch diameter springform cake pan, lightly greased

serves 8

Preheat the oven to 350°F.

Put the egg yolks and sugar in a large bowl and beat for 2 minutes. Add the oil and baking of soda and beat until just combined. Fold in the flour, spices, carrot, and walnuts until combined. The mixture should look quite thick. In a separate grease-free bowl, beat the egg whites with an electric whisk until they form soft peaks then fold them into the cake mixture in 2 batches. Spoon the cake mixture into the prepared cake pan and bake in the preheated oven for 45–50 minutes, until golden and slightly puffed on top. Let the cake cool in the pan for about 10 minutes before turning it out onto a wire rack to cool completely.

To make the frosting, put the cream cheese and butter in a bowl and let them come to room temperature. Add the brown sugar and, using an electric whisk, beat for 5 minutes, until there are no lumps and the beaters leave a trail when turned off. Add the maple syrup a little at a time and beat for a further 2 minutes, until the mixture is smooth and a spreadable consistency. Carefully slice the cooled cake in half and spread the frosting on the bottom layer.

Parsnips make a wonderful soup ingredient, sweet and warming, and preparing them in this way is especially good if they are slightly woody. They have a very distinctive taste which marries well with the sweetness of apples, and the flavors are enhanced by a pinch of spicy curry powder and some fresh thyme. The chorizo recipe makes a thick and unctuous soup; the kind you could wolf down after a long walk or building a snowman in the depths of winter. It's very heavy so a little goes a long way; serve it as a meal in itself—offering it as a starter is likely to leave anyone too stuffed for a follow-up course. Both recipes are just the thing to brighten up a dreary winter's day.

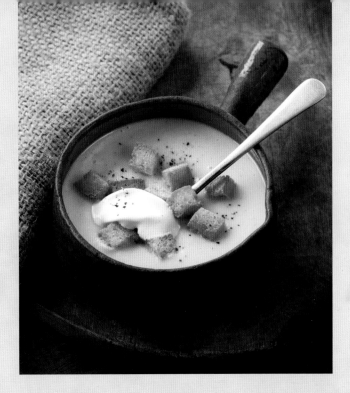

parsnip, chorizo, & chestnut soup

4 oz. raw chorizo, cubed

1 onion, chopped

3 garlic cloves, sliced

1 celery rib, chopped

1 carrot, chopped

3 parsnips, chopped

¼ teaspoon dried hot pepper flakes

1 teaspoon ground cumin

6½ oz. peeled, cooked chestnuts (fresh or vacuum-packed)

4 cups hot chicken or ham stock

sea salt and freshly ground black pepper

serves 4–6

Put the chorizo in a large saucepan and heat gently for 2–3 minutes until the oil seeps out and the chorizo becomes slightly crispy. Lift out the chorizo with a slotted spoon, trying to leave as much oil behind as you can, and set to one side.

Add the onion, garlic, celery, carrot, and parsnips to the pan, stir well, cover, and cook gently for 10 minutes, or until softening. Add the hot pepper flakes and cumin, season with sea salt and freshly ground black pepper, and stir to release the aroma. Add the chestnuts and hot stock, then cover and simmer over low heat for 25–30 minutes until everything is very tender.

Transfer the contents of the pan to a blender (or use a handheld blender) and liquidize until smooth.

Reheat the chorizo in a small skillet. Divide the soup equally between 4–6 bowls, scatter with the crispy chorizo, and serve.

parsnip, apple, & thyme soup

1 small onion, chopped

2 tablespoons olive oil

1 teaspoon mild curry powder

a few sprigs of fresh thyme

1 lb. parsnips (about 2–3), peeled and chopped

1 large tart cooking apple, such as Bramley, peeled, cored, and roughly chopped

5 cups chicken or vegetable stock

1 tablespoon unsalted butter

3 heaping tablespoons crème fraîche or sour cream, plus extra to serve

sea salt and freshly ground black pepper

croûtons, to serve (optional)

serves 4

Put the onions, oil, curry powder, and a good pinch of salt in a large saucepan. Cook gently over low heat until the onions are soft. Add the thyme, parsnips, and apple and stir well. Cook for about 5 minutes, adding a little more oil if it needs it and stirring often. Add the stock and season to taste.

Simmer gently, uncovered, until the parsnips are soft, about 15–20 minutes. Purée the soup with a handheld blender, or by transferring it to a food processor and returning to the saucepan once blended. Taste and adjust the seasoning if necessary.

Stir in the butter and 3 heaping tablespoons crème fraîche and mix well. Ladle the soup into serving bowls and top with croûtons (if using) and a small dollop of crème fraîche.

honey-roast parsnip, carrot, & shallot tart

3 carrots, sliced on the diagonal

3 parsnips, cut into matchsticks

6 shallots, halved or quartered, depending on their size

1 tablespoon runny honey

3 tablespoons olive oil

1 teaspoon salt

½ teaspoon ground black pepper

1 cup grated sharp Cheddar cheese

⅔ cup Greek yogurt

spelt pizza dough crust

1⅔ cups spelt flour

1 teaspoon quick-acting dry yeast

½ teaspoon salt

2 tablespoons olive oil

1 egg

¼ cup warm water

a 9-inch loose-based tart pan, greased

makes about 8 slices

Plenty of roasted winter vegetables with a hint of honey set in a light wholemeal spelt and olive oil crust—this makes a great rustic starter or accompaniment to winter roasts and stews.

Preheat the oven to 400°F.

Put the carrots, parsnips, and shallots in a roasting pan. Add the honey, oil, salt, and pepper and toss until evenly coated. Cover the pan with aluminum foil and roast in the preheated oven for 30 minutes. Remove from the oven, leave covered, and let cool for 10–15 minutes.

Reduce the oven temperature to 325°F.

To make the pastry dough, mix the flour, yeast, and salt in a bowl. Make a well in the centre and pour in the oil, egg, and water. Draw everything together with your hands until you get a soft dough.

Transfer the dough to a lightly floured surface and knead for a couple of minutes. The dough should be soft but not sticky. If it is sticky, add a little flour and knead again. Roll out the dough with a rolling pin until ⅛ inch thick. Line the tart pan with the dough but do not trim the edges yet.

Mix ⅔ cup of the cheese into the roasted vegetables.

Mix together the yogurt and remaining cheese in a bowl, then spoon into the tart crust.

Scatter the roasted vegetables over the yogurt, spreading them evenly. Now trim the excess pizza dough neatly around the edges.

Bake in the hot oven for 25–30 minutes. Remove from the oven and leave to cool.

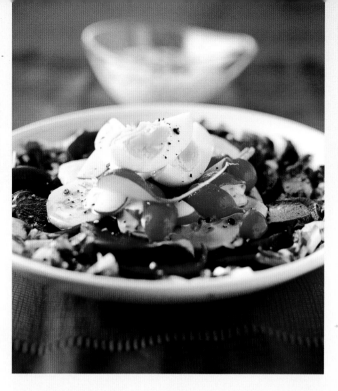

Earthy and fruity, with a hint of ginger, this tagine is a good winter warmer. It can be made with either fresh or pre-cooked beets. You could serve it with roasted butternut squash and a mound of couscous tossed with pistachios. With a summer crop, prepare a pretty cardinals' salad, so called because the colors are reminiscent of a cardinal's ruby-red robes. The sweetness of the beet contrasts well with the bitterness of the radicchio leaves. You could also add some potatoes for a more substantial salad.

beet & beef tagine with oranges

1–2 tablespoons ghee, or 1 tablespoon olive oil plus a pat of butter

3–4 garlic cloves, crushed

1 red onion, halved lengthwise and sliced with the grain

1½-inch piece fresh ginger, peeled and finely chopped or grated

1 red chile, seeded and sliced

2 teaspoons coriander seeds, crushed

2 cinnamon sticks

3–4 beets, peeled and quartered

1 lb. lean beef, cut into bite-sized cubes or strips

2 thin-skinned oranges, cut into segments

1 tablespoon dark, runny honey

1–2 tablespoons orange flower water

a pat of butter

2–3 tablespoons shelled pistachios

leaves from a small bunch of fresh flatleaf parsley, roughly chopped

sea salt and freshly ground black pepper

couscous, to serve

serves 4–6

Melt the ghee in a tagine or heavy-based casserole, add the garlic, onion, and ginger and stir until they begin to color. Add the chile, coriander seeds, and cinnamon sticks. Add the beets and sauté for 2–3 minutes. Toss in the beef and sauté for 1 minute. Pour in enough water to almost cover the beef and beets and bring to a boil. Reduce the heat, cover with a lid, and simmer for 1 hour, until the meat is very tender.

Add the orange segments, honey, and orange flower water to the tagine and season to taste with salt and pepper. Cover with the lid and cook for a further 10–15 minutes.

Melt the butter in a small saucepan and toss in the pistachios, stirring them over medium heat until they turn golden brown. Sprinkle them over the tagine along with the flatleaf parsley and serve immediately with couscous.

cardinal's salad

4 tablespoons mayonnaise

1 tablespoon red wine vinegar or raspberry vinegar

2 tablespoons extra virgin olive oil

3 tablespoons chopped fresh chives

1 head radicchio, shredded

1 lb. cooked beets, thinly sliced

½ cucmber, thinly sliced

a bunch of radishes, quartered

3 eggs, hard-boiled and quartered

freshly ground black pepper

serves 6

Put the mayonnaise, vinegar, and olive oil in a bowl and stir to mix. Stir in half the chives and set aside.

Arrange the shredded radicchio on a serving platter. Add a layer of beets and a spoonful of the mayonnaise dressing. Add a layer of cucumber and another spoonful of dressing.

Top with the radishes, then the eggs. Drizzle over the remaining dressing, sprinkle with black pepper and the remaining chives, and serve.

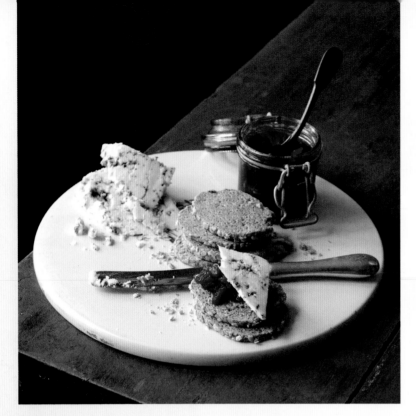

If you have a glut of beets, they make the perfect base for preserves. Sweet, sour, and delicately spiced, this gorgeous chutney is perfect for serving with heavier cheeses and crackers. If you're serving burgers, sausages, or steaks (even salmon steaks), beet & horseradish relish will transform the meal. Fresh, raw beets are best, but you can substitute pre-cooked if you are short on time.

beet, fennel, & apple chutney

5½ oz. cooked beet, cubed

5 oz. fennel, trimmed and cubed

5 oz. sour apple, peeled, cored and cubed

1 small red onion, cubed

¾ cup cider vinegar

1 cup sugar

½ star anise

2 cloves

1 teaspoon salt

2 x 8-oz. jars, sterilized (see note on page 4)

makes two 8-oz. jars

Put all the ingredients in a saucepan and bring to a boil, then cook over low/medium heat for 1 hour, stirring occasionally. If after 1 hour the chutney hasn't reached a jam-like consistency, leave it to cook for up to 20 more minutes.

Spoon the hot chutney into the sterilized jars and seal immediately. Leave for 2–3 days before serving. The chutney will keep in the refrigerator for up to 2 weeks.

beet & horseradish relish

2 tablespoons sugar

2 tablespoons balsamic vinegar

10½ oz. raw beetroot, peeled

1 tablespoon bottled horseradish

makes about 1¼ cups

To make the relish, put the sugar and vinegar in a small saucepan and bring to a boil, stirring. Boil for 1 minute, then remove from the heat. Grate the beetroot into a bowl and combine with the horseradish and vinegar syrup. The relish will keep in the refrigerator for up to 1 week.

* tip

Beets can be enjoyed both raw (they are delicious grated into salads) and cooked. If cooking, always leave the skins on while doing so as this will preserve more of the color and nutrients in the vegetable. After cooking, the thin skins can be easily rubbed off under running water.

mini chocolate, beet, & cherry cakes

2½ oz. bittersweet chocolate (about 50% cocoa solids)

1⅓ cups self-rising flour

⅓ cup cocoa powder

¾ cup light muscovado or packed light brown sugar

1 cup groundnut or vegetable oil

3 large eggs

a pinch of salt

5 oz. cooked, peeled beets

⅓ cup dried sour cherries (or dried cranberries), roughly chopped

a 9-hole petite loaf pan (base measurement of each hole 2½ x 3⅜ inches and 1 inch deep), lined with paper mini-loaf cases

makes 9

Preheat the oven to 350°F.

Break the chocolate into pieces and melt it in a heatproof bowl set over a pan of barely simmering water. Leave to cool slightly.

Sift the flour into an electric mixer (or use a large mixing bowl and an electric whisk). Add the cocoa, sugar, oil, eggs, salt, and the melted chocolate, and whisk until combined. Using the coarse side of a grater, grate the beets into the mixture and sprinkle in the chopped sour cherries. Using a large metal spoon, fold everything together gently.

Divide the mixture between the loaf liners. Bake in the preheated oven for 20–25 minutes, or until well risen. Leave the cakes to cool completely in the pan.

Note The petite loaf pan and matching cases needed for these cakes can be bought from www.wilton.com. If you prefer, you can bake the cakes in muffin cases instead of mini-loaf cases—they will take 25–30 minutes in the oven, and make 9 muffins.

Using beets in these cakes gives them slightly squidgy centres and they freeze well, before decorating. They are also lovely to make as a gift, just dust the tops with cocoa, then sprinkle with edible mini gold balls—dip the end of your finger in a little cold water before applying so that they stick.

bulb & stem vegetables

braised fennel with polenta 🌿 fennel roasted in butter
fennel & lemon risotto 🌿 fennel & tomato focaccia
leek & potato soup 🌿 flamiche
sage buttered baby leeks with chile breadcrumbs
charred leeks with tarator sauce 🌿 grilled asparagus
with baby chorizo 🌿 cream of asparagus soup
asparagus & goat cheese tart 🌿 asparagus tagliatelle
mediterranean stuffed onions with rice
french onion soup 🌿 roasted onions & sausages
crispy onion rings 🌿 braised onions
pickled onions

Don't be too quick to trim away the feathery leaves from fennel bulbs—these can be added to the final stages of a dish or used as a garnish. While smaller, tender bulbs can be eaten raw, the larger, tougher ones are perfect when braised, as here. Or try roasting fennel bulbs in butter, which transforms them into a perfect accompaniment for any roast, especially fish.

braised fennel with polenta

2 large fennel bulbs

¼ cup light olive oil

1 onion, chopped

2 garlic cloves, chopped

1 small red chile, chopped

a handful of fresh flatleaf parsley leaves, roughly chopped

2 tablespoons freshly squeezed lemon juice

2 tablespoons sweet white wine

2 cups vegetable stock

a handful of small black olives

grated pecorino cheese, to serve

creamy polenta

2 cups whole milk

4 cups vegetable stock

1¼ cups instant polenta

3 tablespoons butter

1 cup finely grated pecorino cheese

serves 4

Cut about ¼ inch from the gnarly stem on the bottom of the fennel bulbs. Cut off the fronds, chop finely, and reserve. Cut off and discard all but about ½ inch from the dark green stems. Thinly slice the remaining white fennel bulb lengthwise. Put the oil in a heavy-based saucepan and set over high heat. Add the onion, garlic, and chiles and cook for 2–3 minutes until softened. Add the parsley and fennel bulb and fronds and cook for 2–3 minutes, stirring often so that the fennel becomes coated in the oil. Add the lemon juice, wine, and stock and bring to a boil. Cover with a lid and turn the heat down to a low simmer for 20 minutes, stirring occasionally. Add the olives, remove the lid, and boil rapidly until there is only a little liquid left and the fennel is very soft.

Meanwhile, to make the polenta, put the milk and stock in a saucepan and bring to a gentle simmer over medium heat. Slowly pour in the polenta in a steady stream and beat with a balloon whisk until smooth. Reduce the heat to low and continue to beat for 2–3 minutes. When the mixture thickens, discard the whisk and use a wooden spoon. Add the butter and cheese and stir until melted into the polenta. Spoon some polenta onto serving plates, top with the braised fennel, and sprinkle with grated pecorino to serve.

fennel roasted in butter

3 fennel bulbs

4 tablespoons olive oil or melted butter

sea salt

freshly chopped dill, tarragon or fennel fronds (optional), to serve

serves 6

Trim and remove the stalks and coarse outer leaves from the fennel if necessary. Cut each bulb in half, then each half into 2–3 pieces, depending on size. Slice each piece with a bit of stem or root attached to keep the pieces in place. Reserve any feathery fronds, to chop over the dish just before serving.

Put the fennel in a large saucepan of lightly salted water, bring to a boil, and blanch until nearly tender. Drain and pat dry.

Arrange the pieces in a single layer in a roasting pan, baste with the oil or butter, and cook in a preheated oven at 425°F for about 20 minutes. From time to time, turn them and baste with the oil or butter so they brown evenly on all sides.

To enhance the aniseed flavor, dust with chopped dill, tarragon, or fennel fronds, if using, then serve.

Variation Sprinkle with cheese and cook for a further 5 minutes, then serve as a separate dish or starter.

fennel **37**

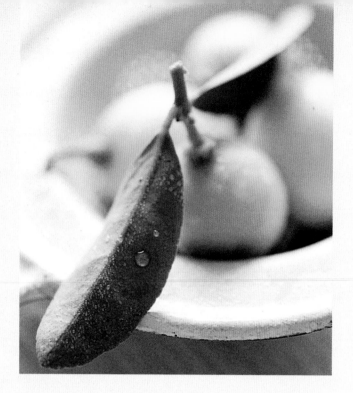

Adding a nip of vodka towards the end of cooking adds a delightful flavor to this fennel & lemon risotto. This recipe is simple to make and always a terrific success with guests. Also great for lunchtime visitors is Focaccia—a rustic-style bread traditionally cooked over an open fire and made for tearing and sharing. If you like this recipe, try it again topped with other ingredients such as red onions, olives, and sprigs of rosemary or thyme.

fennel & tomato focaccia

2 baby fennel bulbs, thinly sliced and fronds chopped

2 tomatoes, thinly sliced

1½ teaspoons sea salt flakes

extra virgin olive oil, to serve

focaccia dough

3⅓ cups white bread flour

1 teaspoon salt

2 teaspoons dried yeast

3 tablespoons olive oil

all-purpose flour, for kneading and dusting

serves 6–8

For the dough, sift the flour and salt into a large bowl and add the yeast. Stir to combine and make a small well in the center. Add 1¼ cups warm water and 2 tablespoons of the olive oil. Quickly stir a few times just to combine, then use your hands to bring the mixture together. (If the mixture is sticking to your hands, add a little flour, but avoid using it if at all possible.) Transfer the dough to a lightly floured work surface and knead for 8–10 minutes, until smooth and elastic. Form the dough into a ball and put it in a lightly oiled bowl. Cover with a kitchen towel and let sit in a warm place for 1½ hours, until doubled in size.

Preheat the oven to 425°F. Put the ball of dough on a lightly oiled baking sheet. Using a lightly floured rolling pin, gently roll from the centre upwards in one motion, not pressing too firmly so that any air bubbles stay intact. Roll from the centre down to the opposite end to form a rough oval shape, about 12 inches long and 8 inches at its widest point. Lightly cover and let sit again for 20–30 minutes until it has risen.

Use the tips of your fingers to press dimples over the surface of the dough. Lay the fennel and tomato slices on top and scatter with the fronds. Drizzle with the remaining olive oil and sprinkle with the salt flakes. Bake in the preheated oven for 25 minutes. Carefully slide the focaccia off the sheet and put it directly on the oven shelf. Cook for a further 5 minutes, until the crust is golden. Remove from the oven and leave to cool before eating. Serve with a small bowl of fruity extra virgin olive oil for dipping.

fennel & lemon risotto

a small pinch of saffron threads

5 cups hot vegetable stock

1 large fennel bulb

1¼ sticks butter

1 onion, chopped

2 garlic cloves

freshly squeezed juice and grated zest of 1 unwaxed lemon

1½ cups risotto rice

½ cup vodka

¼ cup freshly grated Parmesan cheese

sea salt and freshly ground black pepper

serves 4

Soak the saffron in the hot stock until required. Finely chop the fennel bulb and fronds, reserving the fronds.

Melt half the butter in a skillet, add the onion, chopped fennel, garlic, and lemon zest, and fry gently for 10 minutes until softened. Add the rice and stir for 30 seconds until the grains are glossy.

Meanwhile, heat the saffron stock to a gentle simmer. Add a ladle of the stock to the rice and cook, stirring until absorbed. Continue adding the stock a little at a time, stirring, and cook for about 20 minutes until the liquid is absorbed and the rice is al dente (just done).

Remove the pan from the heat, stir in the remaining butter, lemon juice, vodka, Parmesan, reserved fennel fronds, salt, and pepper, cover, leave for 5 minutes, then serve.

Sometimes the classics really are the best, and with both leek and potato soup and a traditional flamiche tart from Belgium, this is certainly true. While the soup is a perfect winter warmer, the tart is ideal for a picnic served with some pâte and cold meats. If your leeks are from the garden, complete with the mud and insects that cohabit with them, place them in a sink full of warm water and swirl them around to dissolve the mud and encourage it to come out.

leek & potato soup

3 tablespoons butter

4 leeks (about 1 lb.), chopped

3 potatoes (about 8 oz.), peeled and chopped

1 onion, finely chopped

2 cups vegetable stock

1¼ cups milk

2 dried bay leaves

2 tablespoons freshly snipped chives, to serve

sea salt and freshly ground black pepper

serves 4–6

Melt the butter in a large, preferably heavy-based saucepan and add the leeks, potatoes, onion, and a large pinch of salt. Cover and cook over low heat for 15 minutes until soft and translucent. Stir occasionally so that the vegetables don't catch.

Add the stock, milk, and bay leaves and bring to a boil. Turn the heat down and simmer, covered, for 20 minutes until the potato is so soft it is falling apart.

Transfer the soup to a blender, removing the bay leaves as you unearth them, and liquidize until smooth. Strain the blended soup back into the pan to get it extra smooth. Bring back to a boil.

Divide the soup between 4–6 bowls and scatter with chives and a fresh grinding of black pepper.

flamiche

12 oz. ready-made shortcrust pastry, at room temperature

6 tablespoons butter

2 lbs. leeks, split, well washed, and thickly sliced

1 teaspoon salt

4 large egg yolks

1¼ cups heavy cream or crème fraîche

freshly grated nutmeg, to taste

sea salt and freshly ground black pepper

an 8-inch diameter tart pan
a baking sheet

foil or baking parchment and baking beans

serves 4–6

Preheat the oven to 400°F.

Roll out the pastry thinly on a lightly floured work surface, then use it to line the tart pan, prick the base, then chill or freeze for 15 minutes. After this time, line the tart crust with foil or baking parchment then fill with baking beans. Bake in the centre of the oven for 10–12 minutes. Remove the foil or parchment paper and baking beans and return the crust to the oven for 5–7 minutes longer to dry out completely.

For the tart filling, melt the butter in a large saucepan and add the leeks, stirring to coat. Add a few tablespoons of water and the 1 teaspoon salt, and cover with a lid. Steam very gently for at least 30 minutes (trying not to look too often!) until soft and melting. Remove the lid and cook for a further few minutes to evaporate any excess liquid—the mixture should be quite thick. Leave to cool.

Put the egg yolks and cream or crème fraîche into a bowl, add salt, pepper, and nutmeg to taste and beat well. Set the pie crust on a baking sheet. Spoon the cooled leeks evenly into the pie crust, fluffing them up a bit with a fork. Pour the eggs and cream mixture over the top.

Bake in the preheated oven for 30 minutes or until set and pale golden brown. Serve warm.

sage buttered baby leeks
with chile breadcrumbs

5 tablespoons salted butter

2 tablespoons finely chopped fresh sage

1 lb. short thin baby leeks, split halfway through and well washed

2 tablespoons extra virgin olive oil

1 scant cup fresh ciabatta breadcrumbs

1 mild long red chile, seeded and finely chopped

1 smaller red chile, seeded and sliced into rings

serves 4

Put the butter and sage in a bowl and mash well.

Steam or boil the leeks for about 5 minutes, or until tender. Toss in half the sage butter and keep hot.

Heat a skillet, add the olive oil and ciabatta breadcrumbs, and fry for about 45 seconds. Add the remaining sage butter and the finely chopped chiles. Fry until golden.

Put the leeks on a serving plate, and top with the chile breadcrumbs and the smaller sliced chile. Serve with other dishes or as a starter.

Note Sea kale and salsify are also good served this way.

Sage makes a great partnership with leeks, and the Italian-style chile breadcrumb topping makes for a delicious combination. For an even more pronounced Italian accent, the crispy breadcrumbs are made from ciabatta bread. Or if you favor a flavor of the Middle Eastern, top grilled leeks with a nut sauce, tarator. This recipe uses macadamias, though traditionally it is prepared with ground almonds or walnuts. If the sauce is made in advance, whisk well before use.

charred leeks
with tarator sauce

1½ lbs. baby leeks, trimmed

2–3 tablespoons extra virgin olive oil

sea salt

a few lemon wedges, to serve

tarator sauce

2 oz. macadamia nuts, toasted

½ cup fresh breadcrumbs

2 garlic cloves, crushed

½ cup extra virgin olive oil

1 tablespoon lemon juice

2 tablespoons boiling water

sea salt and freshly ground black pepper

serves 4

To make the sauce, put the nuts into a food processor and grind coarsely, then add the breadcrumbs, garlic, salt, and pepper and process again to form a smooth paste. Transfer to a bowl and very gradually whisk in the olive oil, lemon juice, and the 2 tablespoons boiling water to form a sauce. Season to taste with salt and pepper.

Preheat an outdoor grill. Brush the leeks with a little olive oil, season with salt, and cook over medium hot coals for 6–10 minutes, turning occasionally, until charred and tender. Transfer to a serving plate, sprinkle with olive oil, then pour the sauce over the top and serve with the lemon wedges.

Asparagus is a vegetable much used in Spanish cuisine, and this heritage is illustrated in these two dishes. Asparagus served with fresh mayonnaise, coarse sea salt, and sautéed sliced baby chorizos is a simple rustic country dish. Asparagus soup has a delicate flavor that goes very well with sherry —try a manzanilla with this dish.

grilled asparagus
with baby chorizo

1½ lbs. thin asparagus
3 tablespoons olive oil
a pinch of fine sea salt
freshly ground black pepper

mayonnaise
1 garlic clove, finely chopped
2 teaspoons freshly squeezed lemon juice
a pinch of salt

1 egg yolk
⅔ cup olive oil

to serve
coarse sea salt
2 baby chorizos (choricitos), sliced, then fried without oil in a dry skillet

serves 4

To make the mayonnaise, put the garlic, half the lemon juice, a pinch of salt, and a few drops of water in a mortar and pound to a paste. Add the egg yolk, grinding with the pestle in one direction. Gradually mix in the oil in drops. After adding ½ cup, add a little more of the lemon juice and continue slowly mixing in the oil until a thick emulsion forms. Taste and adjust the flavor with more salt and the remaining lemon juice if needed. Alternatively, use a blender or small food processor, but you will have to double the ingredients or the mixture won't cover the blades. Cover any leftovers with plastic wrap, chill, and keep for another use.

Trim the asparagus and peel away the papery triangular bits from the stalk. Put the oil, salt, and pepper in a shallow dish, add the asparagus, and turn to coat.

Heat a ridged stove-top grill pan until smoking. Add the asparagus, a batch at a time, turning the spears over when grill marks appear. They will take 1½–2½ minutes on each side. Serve while still hot with the mayonnaise, sea salt, and chorizos in small bowls.

cream of asparagus soup

1½ lbs. asparagus
3 tablespoons olive oil
1 tablespoon butter
2 leeks, well washed and thinly sliced
1 onion, finely chopped

1 quart chicken stock
freshly grated nutmeg
⅔ cup heavy cream
fine sea salt and freshly ground white pepper

serves 4

Cut the tips off 8 asparagus spears and reserve. Chop the remainder into ¾-inch pieces.

Heat the oil and butter in a saucepan, add the leeks and onion, cover, and sauté over gentle heat for 10 minutes. Add the chopped asparagus, stock, grated nutmeg, season well with salt and pepper, and simmer for 10 minutes.

Transfer to a blender, purée until smooth, then, using the back of a ladle, push through a sieve set over a bowl. Alternatively, use a mouli. Add two-thirds of the cream to the bowl and stir well. Return the soup to the saucepan and heat gently when ready to serve (do not let boil).

Cook the reserved asparagus tips in boiling water until just tender. Ladle the soup into bowls, spoon the remaining cream on top, add the asparagus tips and some more nutmeg, then serve.

There must be something extremely special about asparagus for it to survive being called names like "chambermaids' horror" and "sparrows' guts"! Young asparagus is one of life's great gifts, but be careful not to miss its short seasonal window. Because it is such a treat, keep it simple. Of course it is wonderful blanched and served with hollandaise, but why not try combining the prime spears with a handful of other fresh, good-quality ingredients. The fresh, crunchy spears are a perfect foil for rich ingredients, such as the goat cheese in this tart or in a creamy pasta.

asparagus & goat cheese tart

2 x 12-oz. sheets ready-rolled puff pastry, defrosted if frozen

1 egg, lightly beaten and mixed with 2 teaspoons water

2 tablespoons butter

2 tablespoons light olive oil

2 bunches thin asparagus, woody ends trimmed

5 oz. soft goat cheese

sea salt and freshly ground black pepper

2 baking sheets, lined with baking parchment

serves 4

Preheat the oven to 425°F.

Cut the sheets of pastry to make two rectangles 10 x 5 inches and place each one on a baking sheet lined with baking parchment. Cut ½-inch wide strips from the remaining pastry. Brush around the edges of the pastry rectangles and place the strips on the edges to form a border. Prick the centre of each pastry with a fork and brush the beaten egg all over it. Cook in the preheated oven for 15 minutes, until pale golden and puffed.

Put the butter and olive oil in a skillet over high heat and cook the asparagus for 2–3 minutes, turning often, until just beginning to soften. Season well with sea salt and black pepper and set aside. Crumble the goat cheese over the pastry, staying within the borders. Top with the asparagus and cook in the oven for a further 10 minutes until the pastry is dark golden. Serve warm.

asparagus tagliatelle

1 cup light cream

10 oz. tagliatelle pasta, or simliar

1 bunch of fine asparagus, trimmed and each spear cut into 4

grated zest and freshly squeezed juice of 1 unwaxed lemon

3 tablespoons finely chopped fresh flatleaf parsley

1 cup finely grated Parmesan cheese

sea salt and freshly ground black pepper

serves 4, as a starter

Put the cream in a small saucepan and bring to a boil. Reduce the heat to a low simmer and cook for 8–10 minutes, until slightly thickened. Set aside.

Cook the pasta according to the packet instructions. About 2 minutes before the pasta is cooked, add the asparagus to the boiling water. Drain well and return to the warm pan with the reduced cream, lemon zest and juice, parsley, and half of the Parmesan. Toss together, season well with sea salt and black pepper, and serve with the remaining Parmesan sprinkled on top.

Variation As a substitute to asparagus, pan-fry 1 grated zucchini in 1 tablespoon of butter over medium heat until softened and golden. Add the zucchini to the well-drained pasta along with the other ingredients.

Onions are easy to grow in abundance and these recipes make sure you get through plenty of them. Both dishes are warming and comforting. Onions make a nifty, and tasty, container for the gently spiced lamb filling. Rich French onion soup, topped with melting cheese toasts is synonymous with bistro eating. This recipe is a simplified version, the sort of thing that's ideal when it's chilly outside, people are hungry inside, and there's not much more than a few onions lurking about.

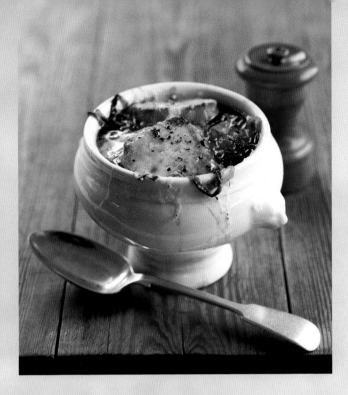

mediterranean stuffed onions with rice

8 large red or white onions

2–3 tablespoons olive oil

1 lb. ground lamb

2 garlic cloves, crushed

1 heaping tablespoon tomato paste

½ cup dry white wine

½ teaspoon ground cinnamon

2 tablespoons finely chopped fresh dill

2 tablespoons finely chopped fresh mint

1½ cups brown rice

1 cup fresh breadcrumbs

1 egg, beaten

sea salt and freshly ground black pepper

serves 4

Slice the tops and bottoms off of the onions, taking only a little at the root end and more at the top. Scoop out the insides, leaving 2–3 layers of the outer onion as a shell. Put the scooped-out onion flesh in a food processor and process until finely chopped.

Put 1 tablespoon of the oil in a skillet and add 4 tablespoons of the chopped onions. Cook for 3–5 minutes, until soft. Add the lamb, season well, and cook for 5–7 minutes, stirring to break up the meat. Stir in the garlic, tomato paste, wine, cinnamon, dill, and mint and cook for 2–3 minutes, stirring. Taste and adjust the seasoning. Remove from the heat and let cool.

Preheat the oven to 400°F. Add the rice in an even layer in the bottom of the baking dish. Brush the inside of the onion shells with oil and sprinkle with salt.

When the stuffing is cool enough to handle, stir in the breadcrumbs, egg, and 2–3 tablespoons water. The mixture should be soft, but not soupy. Spoon the mixture into the onion shells, filling all the way to the top. Arrange the filled onions on top of the rice and brush the outsides with oil. Pour 2 cups water into the dish.

Bake in the preheated oven for 1–1½ hours, until the rice is cooked. Keep an eye on the rice and begin testing it after 1 hour in the oven. You may need to add more water. Serve immediately or let cool and serve with a mixed green salad on the side.

french onion soup

3 tablespoons unsalted butter

1 tablespoon olive oil

3 large onions (about 3 lbs.) thinly sliced

2 garlic cloves, crushed

1 tablespoon all-purpose flour

1 quart beef, chicken, or vegetable stock

2¾ cups dry white wine

1 fresh bay leaf

2 sprigs of fresh thyme

1 baguette, sliced

1½ cups grated Gruyère cheese (about 5 oz.)

coarse sea salt and freshly ground black pepper

serves 4–6

Put the butter and oil in a large saucepan and melt over medium heat. Add the onions and cook over low heat for 15–20 minutes, until soft.

Add the garlic and flour and cook, stirring, for about 1 minute. Add the stock, wine, bay leaf, and thyme. Season with salt and pepper and bring to a boil. Boil for 1 minute, then lower the heat and simmer very gently for 20 minutes. Taste and adjust the seasoning. At this point, the soup will be cooked, but standing time will improve the flavor—at least 30 minutes.

Before serving, preheat the broiler. Put the baguette slices on a baking sheet and brown under the broiler until lightly toasted. Set aside. Do not turn the broiler off.

To serve, ladle the soup into ovenproof bowls and top with a few toasted baguette rounds. Sprinkle cheese over the top and cook under the broiler until browned and bubbling. Serve immediately.

roasted onions & sausages

3 white or red onions (or a mixture of both), cut into wedges

olive oil, to drizzle

4 eating apples

12 good-quality chipolatas or other sausages

serves 4

Preheat the oven to 400°F.

Scatter the onions over a heavy-based roasting pan. Drizzle over a little olive oil.

Core the apples and cut them into quarters. Add to the roasting pan, top with the sausages, and drizzle with a little more olive oil. Roast in the preheated oven for about 25–30 minutes, turning halfway through.

crispy onion rings

two red onions, thinly sliced

two white onions, thinly sliced

1 cup buttermilk

6 tablespoons chickpea flour

6 tablespoons cornstarch

1 teaspoon sea salt

2 eggs

2 cups vegetable oil

serves 4

Put the onion slices in a large bowl and gently toss to separate the rings. Add the buttermilk and stir. Set aside for 1 hour.

Put the chickpea flour, cornstarch, and salt in a bowl. Make a well in the centre. Use a slotted spoon to remove the onions from the buttermilk (reserving the buttermilk) and transfer them to a colander to drain off any excess liquid. Put ½ cup of the reserved buttermilk in a bowl and beat in the eggs until just combined. Pour this mixture into the flour mixture and beat well to form a smooth, thick batter.

Put the oil in a skillet set over medium/high heat. Toss a handful of onion rings into the batter and lift them out with a slotted spoon (letting any excess batter drip back into the bowl). Put them in the skillet. Cook for about 1 minute, or until golden. Remove from the oil with a slotted spoon and drain on paper towels. Repeat with the remaining onion rings. Serve warm.

Pictured with Potato & Parsnip Croquettes – recipe on page 11.

braised onions

1½ lbs. small onions

4 tablespoons olive oil

4 garlic cloves, peeled and halved lengthwise

a sprig of bay leaves

1 teaspoon smoked sweet paprika (pimentón dulce)

4 tablespoons dry white wine

coarse sea salt and freshly ground black pepper

serves 4

Peel the onions, but leave the root end on.

Heat the oil in a heavy or cast iron enamelled heatproof casserole with a lid. Add the onions, garlic and bay leaves and cook over medium heat for 5 minutes. Stir often to stop them browning.

Add the paprika, salt, pepper, and wine, cover and cook slowly until just tender, about 25 minutes (however, they can take up to 45 minutes depending on size).

pickled onions

3 tablespoons salt

1 lb. shallots or pickling onions

spiced vinegar

8 mixed peppercorns

4 whole cloves

½-inch cinnamon stick

½-inch piece fresh ginger

1¾ cups malt vinegar

1 pint preserving jar, sterilized (see note on page 4)

makes 1 pint

To make a brine, put the salt in a saucepan with 2¾ cups water. Bring to a boil, remove from the heat, and let cool.

Peel the shallots and put them in a bowl, add the cooled brine and leave for 24 hours. After this time, drain, rinse in cold water, and dry.

To make the spiced vinegar, put the peppercorns, cloves, cinnamon, and ginger in a small saucepan. Add the vinegar, cover, and bring to a boil over low heat. Turn off the heat, let cool, then strain.

Pack the onions into the jar, pushing them down with the handle of a wooden spoon. Top up with the cooled spiced vinegar. Tap the sides to remove any air bubbles or slide a thin knife blade down the inside of the jar to release them. Cover with a waxed paper disc or baking parchment, seal the jar, and store in a cool, dark cupboard until required. Wait at least 3 months before tasting.

fruiting vegetables

baked stuffed eggplant 🌿 griddled eggplant with lemon
& mint 🌿 **eggplant, red bell pepper, & tomato tart**
moussaka 🌿 **pan-grilled eggplant with honey & spices**
fiery red bell pepper soup 🌿 **red bell pepper scones**
three bell pepper tagine with eggs 🌿 **grilled bell pepper,
tomato, & chile salad** 🌿 roasted red bell pepper & walnut dip
smoky pepper & eggplant salsa 🌿 crunchy bell pepper
& corn relish 🌿 **casablancan stuffed tomatoes**
slow-cooked tomatoes with goat cheese & garlic toasts
triple tomato & basil risotto 🌿 roast tomato ketchup
upside-down tomato tart 🌿 tomato soup
tomato, mozzarella, & basil salad 🌿 chile tomato jam
roasted tomatoes 🌿 corn, asparagus, &
goat cheese frittata 🌿 **corn, zucchini, & cumin soup**
grilled corn with chile lime butter
corn & sun-dried tomato corn bread 🌿 tagine of artichokes,
potatoes, & peas 🌿 **pan-fried artichokes with thyme & ricotta**

Versatile and filling, eggplant can be used in many ways, and makes a great vegetarian alternative. This dish of baked stuffed eggplant can be served as a course on its own or as a side dish to roasted and grilled meats. The harissa (see note on page 59) adds a wonderful touch of warmth. Serve with chunks of crusty bread to mop up the delicious juices.

baked stuffed eggplant

2 eggplants, halved lengthwise

2–3 tablespoons olive oil, plus extra for drizzling

1 onion, chopped

2 tomatoes, skinned and chopped plus 1 tomato, skinned and thinly sliced

½ cup fresh breadcrumbs, toasted

2 garlic cloves, crushed

a small bunch of fresh cilantro, chopped

1–2 teaspoons harissa paste

1 teaspoon sugar

sea salt and freshly ground black pepper

serves 4

Preheat the oven to 350ºF. Using a spoon, scoop out the eggplant flesh and place it on a chopping board. Brush the insides of the empty eggplant shells with a little olive oil, place them on a baking sheet, and bake them in the oven for 4–5 minutes.

Meanwhile, coarsely chop the eggplant flesh. Heat the remaining oil in a skillet and fry the onions to soften. Add the eggplant flesh, cook for a few minutes more, then stir in the tomatoes. Add the breadcrumbs, garlic, cilantro, harissa, and sugar. Season to taste with salt and pepper.

Spoon the mixture into the empty eggplant shells. Arrange the slices of tomato on the top of each one, drizzle with a little olive oil, and bake in the preheated oven for 20–25 minutes. Serve hot.

Although simplicity itself to make, the success of this dish relies on griddling the eggplant perfectly. There is nothing worse than undercooked eggplant, so make sure you baste with plenty of oil, and don't let the pan get too hot or the eggplant will burn before they brown—they should gently sizzle. Add a little crushed or chopped garlic to the dressing if you like, but the mint and lemon flavors are quite delicate so show restraint.

griddled eggplant with lemon & mint

2 medium eggplants (about 14 oz.)

olive oil, for basting

dressing

⅔ cup extra virgin olive oil

finely grated zest and freshly squeezed juice of 1 lemon

2 tablespoons balsamic vinegar

1–2 teaspoons sugar

4 tablespoons very coarsely chopped fresh mint

sea salt and freshly ground black pepper

a ridged stove-top griddle pan or outdoor grill

serves 4

To make the dressing, put the oil, lemon zest and juice, and balsamic vinegar in a bowl and whisk well. Add the sugar, salt, and pepper to taste—it should be fairly sweet. Stir in half the mint, then set aside.

Heat a ridged stove-top grill pan until hot or light an outdoor grill and wait for the coals to turn white. Cut each eggplant lengthwise into 8 thin slices, brush liberally with olive oil, add to the pan or grill, and cook for 2–3 minutes on each side, until golden brown and lightly charred. Arrange the slices on a large platter and spoon the dressing over the top.

Cover and set aside so that the eggplant absorbs the flavors of the dressing. Sprinkle with the remaining chopped mint and serve warm or at room temperature.

This deliciously easy tart is packed full of juicy summer vegetables. It's a great choice for a sophisticated picnic with friends.

eggplant, red bell pepper, & tomato tart

5¾ oz. baby eggplant, halved lengthwise (or normal eggplant, chopped)

2 large red bell peppers, seeded and cut into strips

1 large red onion, thinly sliced

3 tablespoons olive oil, plus extra to drizzle

1 teaspoon salt

½ teaspoon crushed black pepper

⅔ cup cherry tomatoes, halved

1 tablespoon chopped fresh parsley

1 cup freshly grated sharp Cheddar cheese

⅔ cup Greek yogurt

pizza dough base

1⅔ cups bread flour

1 teaspoon quick-acting dry yeast

½ teaspoon salt

2 tablespoons olive oil

1 egg

⅓ cup warm water

a 9-inch loose-based fluted tart pan, greased

makes about 8 slices

Preheat the oven to 350°F.

Put the eggplant, bell peppers, and onion in a roasting pan (preferably non-stick), drizzle with oil, and season with the salt and pepper. Cover the roasting pan with aluminum foil. Bake in the preheated oven for about 20 minutes, or until just soft. Remove from the oven and leave to cool, then chop the eggplant flesh (if you haven't already done so). Drain any excess juice from the roasted vegetables.

Reduce the oven temperature to 325°F.

To make the dough base, mix the flour, yeast, and salt in a bowl. Make a well in the centre and pour in the oil, egg, and water. Draw everything together with your hands until you get a soft dough.

Transfer the dough to a lightly floured work surface and knead for a couple of minutes. The dough should be soft but not sticky. If it is sticky, add a little flour and knead again. Roll out the dough with a rolling pin until ⅛ inch thick. Line the tart pan with the dough but do not trim the edges yet. Set aside.

Stir the tomatoes, parsley, and half the cheese into the roasted vegetables and set aside.

In a separate bowl, mix together the yogurt and remaining cheese, then spoon into the tart crust.

Scatter the roasted vegetable mixture evenly over the yogurt. Now trim the excess pizza dough neatly around the edges. Bake in the oven for 25–30 minutes. Remove from the oven and let cool.

* tip

Plenty of oil is required when cooking eggplant as it draws the heat inside the vegetable to aid cooking and also keeps it moist. Salting eggplants before you begin cooking with them means that their spongy flesh absorbs less oil and you get a healthier, less-greasy result. Dissolve a handful of salt in a bowl of cold water and add the sliced or diced eggplant to it. Set a lid or plate on top to keep them submerged and leave for about an hour to draw out the bitter juices. After this time, tip into a colander, rinse, and pat dry with paper towels. You can then use the eggplant as directed in the recipe.

Some recipes for traditional Greek moussaka call for potatoes alongside the eggplant, and some have potatoes only. This one is all eggplant. Another departure here is the yogurt topping in place of the classic béchamel sauce, which makes for a lighter dish. The moussaka improves over time so is best made a day in advance, refrigerated, and baked when ready to serve. The Moroccan-style pan-grilled eggplant is bursting with spicy and fruity flavors— simple to prepare, it packs a real flavor-punch.

moussaka

1 onion, chopped

4–5 tablespoons olive oil

1 lb. grounf lamb

2 garlic cloves, finely chopped

½ teaspoon ground allspice

¼ teaspoon ground cinnamon

2 teaspoons dried oregano

½ cup red wine

2 x 14-oz. cans chopped tomatoes

1 bay leaf, plus extra to garnish

a pinch of sugar

3 medium eggplants, sliced into ½-inch rounds

sea salt and freshly ground black pepper

for the topping

1½ cups Greek yogurt

2 eggs, beaten

6 oz. feta, crumbled

a large handful of fresh mint leaves, chopped

3 tablespoons freshly grated Parmesan cheese

a 12 x 8 inch baking dish

serves 6

Combine the onion and 1 tablespoon of the oil in a large skillet. Cook the onion for about 3–5 minutes, until soft. Add the lamb, season well, and cook, stirring, for about 5 minutes, until browned. Add the garlic, allspice, cinnamon, and oregano and cook for 1 minute. Add the wine and cook for 1 minute more. Add the tomatoes, bay leaf, and sugar and mix well. Let simmer gently, uncovered, while you prepare the eggplants.

Preheat the oven to 400°F.

Heat a few tablespoons of the oil in a large non-stick skillet. Add the eggplant slices in a single layer and cook to brown slightly. Using tongs, turn and cook the other sides, then transfer to paper towels to drain. Work in batches, adding more oil as necessary, until all the eggplant slices are browned.

In a bowl, combine the yogurt, eggs, and feta and mix well with a fork until blended. Season well with salt and pepper and stir in the mint. Set aside.

To assemble the moussaka, arrange half of the lamb mixture on the bottom of the baking dish. Top with half of the eggplant slices. Repeat once more. Spread the yogurt mixture on top and level the surface. Sprinkle with the Parmesan and decorate with bay leaves. Bake in the preheated oven for about 40–50 minutes, until golden brown and bubbling. Serve immediately.

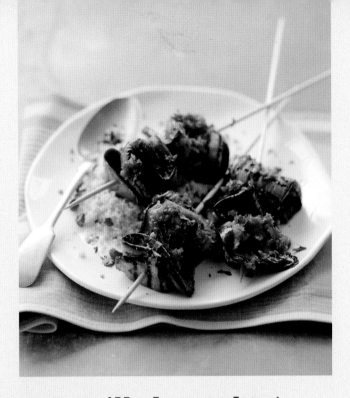

pan-grilled eggplant
with honey & spices

8 eggplants, thickly sliced lengthwise

olive oil, for brushing

2–3 cloves garlic, crushed

a thumb-sized piece of fresh ginger, peeled and crushed

1 teaspoon ground cumin

1 teaspoon harissa paste*

5 tablespoons runny honey

freshly squeezed juice of 1 lemon

sea salt

a small bunch of fresh flatleaf parsley, finely chopped

couscous, to serve

4 metal or wooden skewers, to serve (optional)

serves 4

Brush each eggplant slice with olive oil and cook them on a ridged stove-top grill pan or under the broiler, turning them over so that they are lightly browned.

In a wok or large heavy skillet, fry the garlic in a little olive oil, then stir in the ginger, cumin, harissa, honey, and lemon juice. Add a little water to thin it, then place the eggplant slices in the liquid and cook gently for about 10 minutes, until they have absorbed the sauce. Add more water if necessary and season to taste with salt.

Thread the eggplant onto the skewers, if using, and garnish with the parsley. Serve hot or at room temperature as meal on their own with couscous, or as an accompaniment to grilled meat.

***Note** Harissa is a fiercely hot red chile paste from North Africa, where it is used extensively as a condiment and diluted with stock, water, or fresh tomato sauce to flavor couscous dishes, soups, and tagines.

fiery red bell pepper soup

6 medium red bell peppers
6 carrots (about 1 lb.)
1–2 fresh red chiles
1½ lbs. ripe plum tomatoes
3 large garlic cloves, peeled
6 tablespoons olive oil
2 teaspoons smoked sweet paprika (pimentón dulce)

5 cups vegetable or beef stock
sea salt and freshly ground black pepper
crispy fried bacon slices, to serve

serves 8

Preheat the oven to 400°F.

Cut the stalk ends off the bell peppers, halve and scrape out the seeds. Scrape the carrots and cut into chunky fingers.

If using chiles, cut off the stalks, cut in half, and scrape out the seeds (using rubber gloves if you like).

Put the bell peppers, carrots, chiles, tomatoes, and garlic in large roasting pans so the vegetables aren't too cramped, then toss them in the olive oil. Season well with salt and pepper and roast in the preheated oven for about 30 minutes, until all the vegetables are soft and slightly charred at the edges.

Transfer half the vegetables to a blender, add the paprika and half the stock, and blend until smooth. Pour into a saucepan and repeat with the remaining vegetables and stock, adding extra stock if it seems too thick. Reheat until almost boiling, add salt and pepper to taste, then serve with the bacon crumbled over the top.

This fiery soup will add heat to your belly on a cold day! But if you are making it for children, omit the chiles and use 2 cups milk mixed with 2 cups stock. The perfect accompaniment to the soup is a delicious red bell pepper scone. The secret with scones is just to make them nice and thick. Serve these warm with butter—they are irresistible.

red bell pepper scones

1¾ cups self-rising flour
3 tablespoons butter, diced
1 teaspoon baking powder
1 tablespoon freshly chopped rosemary, plus 10 small sprigs
3½ oz. roasted red bell peppers, drained and finely chopped

1 egg
3 tablespoons milk, plus extra to glaze

makes 10–12

Preheat the oven to 425°F.

Mix the flour and butter in a food processor or with your fingertips until it resembles crumbs. Mix in the baking powder, chopped rosemary, a pinch of salt, and the peppers. Beat the egg with the milk, then pour into the flour, stirring with a knife until you have a smooth dough. Roll out the dough on a lightly floured work surface so it is at least ¾ inch thick and cut out 2-inch circles. Keep rerolling until you have 10–12 scones. Push the rosemary sprigs into the tops, place on a baking sheet, brush with milk, and bake for 15 minutes until golden.

Juicy, sweet, sun-ripened bell peppers feature heavily in the cuisine of Morocco. The gentle aromatic spicing of this cooked salad is just perfect for a warm summer evening. The tagine is one of those dishes you'll find in Morocco at street stalls, bus stations, and working men's cafes. Quick, easy and colorful, it is a great dish for lunch or a tasty snack. Serve either dish with warmed flat breads or pita bread.

three bell pepper tagine with eggs

2 tablespoons olive oil or ghee

1 onion, halved lengthwise and sliced

2–3 garlic cloves, chopped

1–2 teaspoons coriander seeds

1 teaspoon cumin seeds

3 bell peppers (green, red, and yellow), seeded and cut into slices

2 tablespoons green olives, pitted and finely sliced

sea salt and freshly ground black pepper

4–6 very fresh eggs

1 teaspoon paprika or dried hot pepper flakes

leaves from a small bunch of fresh flatleaf parsley, coarsely chopped

warmed flatbreads, to serve

serves 4–6

Heat the olive oil in the base of a tagine, flameproof baking dish, or heavy-based skillet. Add the onions, garlic, coriander and cumin seeds, and sauté, stirring, until the onions begin to soften. Toss in the peppers and olives and sauté until they begin to color. Season well with salt and pepper.

Using your spoon, push aside the peppers to form little pockets for the eggs. Crack the eggs in the pockets and cover for 4–5 minutes until the eggs are cooked. Scatter the paprika over the top and sprinkle with the parsley. Serve immediately from the tagine or pan, with warmed flatbread on the side.

grilled bell pepper, tomato, & chile salad

2 green bell peppers

3–4 long sweet bell peppers

14 oz. ripe tomatoes, skinned (see note on page 69)

¼ teaspoon smoked sweet paprika (pimentón dulce)

¼ teaspoon ground cumin

1 tablespoon freshly squeezed lemon juice

2 tablespoons olive oil

2 tablespoons sliced pickled Jalapeño chiles, rinsed and finely chopped

1 heaped tablespoon finely chopped parsley

sea salt and freshly ground black pepper

serves 6

To peel the bell peppers, either lay them over a low gas flame, turning frequently until the skins char, or halve them, lay them skin-side upwards on a broiler pan and broil under high heat until the skins are blackened. Put the charred peppers in a bowl and cover with plastic wrap (the trapped steam helps to loosen the skins). Once the peppers are cool, the skins should peel off easily.

Seed the peppers, slice them thickly, and put in a serving bowl with the tomatoes. Measure the paprika and cumin into another small bowl and whisk in the lemon juice and oil. Season to taste with salt and pepper. Pour the dressing over the peppers, add the Jalapeños and parsley, and toss together.

This is a traditional Syrian dip called muhammara. There it would be served as part of a meze selection, with hoummus, eggplant dip (baba ganoush), olives, pickles, cheese, and flatbreads. It also works well as a spooning sauce to serve with baked or grilled fish or lamb. It's perfect for entertaining as it benefits from being made a day in advance.

roasted red bell pepper & walnut dip

Cook the peppers one at a time by skewering each one on a fork and holding it directly over a gas flame for 10–15 minutes, until the skin is blackened all over. Alternatively, put them on a baking sheet and then in an oven preheated to 425°F. Cook them for about 10–15 minutes, until the skin has puffed up and blackened all over. Transfer to a bowl, cover with a kitchen towel, and leave until cool enough to handle.

Using your hands, remove the skin and seeds from the peppers and tear the flesh into pieces. (Avoid rinsing with water, as this will remove the smoky flavor.) Put it in a food processor and add the remaining ingredients. Process to a coarse paste. Season to taste with salt and pepper and transfer to a bowl. Cover with plastic wrap and refrigerate for 8 hours or ideally overnight to allow the flavors to fully develop.

To serve, bring the dip to room temperature and transfer it to a shallow bowl. Drizzle with olive oil and sprinkle with chopped pistachios. Serve with torn toasted flatbreads. It will keep in an airtight container in the refrigerator for 4–5 days.

3 large red bell peppers

1 slice of day-old sourdough bread, cut into small pieces

⅔ cup walnut halves, coarsely chopped

½ teaspoon dried hot pepper flakes

1 tablespoon sun-dried tomato paste

2 garlic cloves, chopped

2 teaspoons freshly squeezed lemon juice

1 tablespoon balsamic vinegar

2 teaspoons sugar

1 teaspoon ground cumin

2 tablespoons olive oil, plus extra to serve

chopped pistachios, to sprinkle

sea salt and freshly ground black pepper

toasted flatbread, roughly torn, to serve

serves 6–8

Sweet bell peppers form a great base for condiments to serve with all types of food. This smoky-flavored bell pepper and eggplant salsa is great with grilled food, especially as a flavor-boost on burgers and sausages. Teamed with fresh corn, colorful bell peppers make a vibrant relish, and the crunchy texture also adds appeal. You can serve the relish the day you make it, but it's even better preserved.

smoky bell pepper & eggplant salsa

2 red bell peppers

1 eggplant

3 tablespoons olive oil

1 red onion, finely chopped

3 garlic cloves, chopped

1–2 teaspoons minced red chile

1 teaspoon sugar

½ teaspoon sea salt

1 tablespoon freshly squeezed lemon juice

a small bunch of fresh flatleaf parsley, chopped

2 tablespoons freshly chopped dill

2 teaspoons ground sumac*

makes about 2½ cups

Roast the eggplant and red bell peppers directly over the flame of a gas burner, or put under a preheated broiler, turning regularly, until completely blackened and soft. Put them in a large bowl, cover with a lid or plastic wrap, and let them steam for 10 minutes. Remove and peel off all the blackened skin and discard. Remove the stems and seeds from the bell peppers and chop the flesh very finely. Cut the stem off the eggplant and chop the flesh very finely.

Heat 1 tablespoon of the oil in a skillet, add the onion and garlic, and sauté for 5 minutes until soft. Transfer to a large bowl with the bell peppers, eggplant, remaining oil, chile, sugar, salt, lemon juice, parsley, and dill and mix well. Place in a serving bowl and sprinkle with the sumac. The salsa will keep in the refrigerator for 3 days.

*Note Sumac is a spice widely used in Turkish, Lebanese, and Iranian cooking. The red berries have an astringent quality with a pleasing sour-fruit flavor. They are used whole, but ground sumac is available from Middle Eastern grocers or specialist online retailers.

crunchy bell pepper & corn relish

3 bell peppers (1 red, 1 yellow, and 1 orange)

corn kernels from 2 ears of corn

1 red or white onion, chopped

4 tablespoons sea salt

1 teaspoon white mustard seeds

½ teaspoon cumin seeds

½ teaspoon coriander seeds

½ teaspoon whole black peppercorns

6 small dried chiles

1½ cups white (distilled) vinegar

½ cup plus 1 tablespoon sugar

¼ teaspoon ground turmeric

makes about 3½ cups

Remove the stems from the bell peppers and discard. Cut the bell peppers into 1-inch cubes and put in a colander with the corn and onion. Toss with the salt and leave for 2–4 hours. Rinse well with cold water and shake dry.

Heat a saucepan over medium heat and add the mustard, cumin and coriander seeds, peppercorns, and chiles. Cook, stirring, for 1 minute until fragrant. Add the vinegar, sugar, and turmeric and bring to a boil, stirring to dissolve the sugar.

Add the rinsed corn, bell peppers, and onion to the vinegar mixture. Cover and bring to a boil.

If using immediately, let cool, stirring occasionally. To preserve, fill sterilized jars with the relish while it is still hot and seal (see note on page 4). The relish will keep for up to 2 months if sealed correctly.

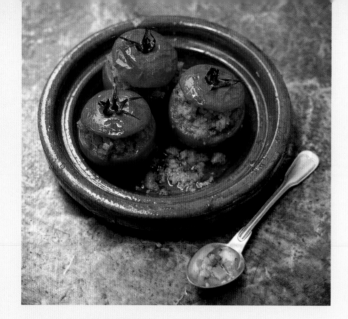

Nothing sings of summer quite like ripe, juicy tomatoes, baked until they become sweet. In Casablanca, these tomatoes stuffed with couscous and herbs are popular as a starter, or they are served on their own with a salad. For both recipes here, it's crucial to use super-ripe tomatoes.

casablancan stuffed tomatoes

¾ cup couscous

½ teaspoon salt

⅔ cup warm water

3–4 tablespoons olive oil, plus extra for drizzling

4 large tomatoes

1 onion, finely chopped

1 carrot, peeled and cubed

a sprinkling of sugar

1–2 teaspoons ras-el-hanout

a bunch each of fresh flatleaf parsley and cilantro, finely chopped

½ preserved lemon, finely chopped

sea salt and freshly ground black pepper

serves 4

Preheat the oven to 350°F.

Put the couscous in a bowl. Stir the salt into the warm water and pour it over the couscous, stirring all the time so that the water is absorbed evenly. Leave the couscous to swell for about 10 minutes before using your fingers to rub 1 tablespoon of the oil into the couscous grains to break up the lumps and aerate them.

Slice the top off each tomato and set aside. Using a spoon, scoop out the pulp and seeds and reserve in a bowl. In a heavy-based saucepan, heat the remaining olive oil and stir in the onion and carrot. Fry until they begin to caramelize, then stir in the tomato pulp and sugar. Add the ras-el-hanout and cook until the mixture forms a thick sauce. Season to taste with salt and pepper.

Tip the spicy tomato mixture onto the couscous and mix well. Add the fresh herbs and preserved lemon and toss until it is thoroughly combined. Spoon the couscous into each tomato cavity and place a top on each one like a lid. Put the filled tomatoes in a baking dish, drizzle with a little olive oil, and bake in the preheated oven for about 25 minutes. Serve hot or leave to cool and eat at room temperature.

slow-cooked tomatoes with goat cheese & garlic toasts

2 cups extra virgin olive oil

1 sprig of fresh oregano

2 teaspoons finely chopped fresh flatleaf parsley leaves

6 very ripe Roma tomatoes

½ teaspoon sea salt

7 oz. soft goat cheese

1 small baguette

2 garlic cloves, peeled

serves 4

Preheat the oven to 250°F.

Put the oil in a small, non-reactive baking dish. Add the oregano and parsley. Cut the tomatoes in half and arrange them in a single layer in the dish. Ideally you want the tomatoes to be almost fully submerged in the oil. Sprinkle the salt evenly over the tomatoes. Cook in the preheated oven for about 5 hours, until the tomatoes are intensely red and softened yet still retain their shape. Remove from the oven and leave the tomatoes in the oil to cool completely.

Put the goat cheese in a serving bowl.

Preheat the broiler. Slice the baguette very thinly. Toast the bread on both sides until golden and crisp and rub one side with the peeled garlic cloves.

Remove the tomatoes from the oil and arrange them on a serving platter with the goat cheese and garlic toasts on the side.

triple tomato & basil risotto

1 lb. whole baby plum tomatoes

4 tablespoons olive oil

about 1 quart hot vegetable stock

2 cups passata (Italian puréed, strained tomatoes)

1 stick unsalted butter

1 onion, finely chopped

8 pieces sun-dried tomatoes (not the ones in oil), chopped

2 cups risotto rice, preferably vialone nano

⅔ cup light red wine

½ cup freshly grated Parmesan cheese

4 tablespoons chopped fresh basil

sea salt and freshly ground black pepper

extra basil leaves, to serve

freshly grated Parmesan cheese, to serve

serves 4

Put the plum tomatoes in a roasting pan and pour over the olive oil. Mix them well to coat and season with salt and pepper. Roast in a preheated oven at 400°F for about 20 minutes or until they are slightly collapsed and the skins beginning to brown. Remove from the oven and set aside.

Pour the stock and passata into a saucepan, stir well, then heat to a gentle simmer. Melt half the butter in a large, heavy saucepan and add the onion and chopped sun-dried tomatoes. Cook gently for 10 minutes until soft, golden and translucent but not browned. Add the rice and stir until well coated with the butter and heated through. Pour in the wine and boil hard until it has reduced and almost disappeared. This will remove the taste of raw alcohol. Remove from the heat.

Return the risotto to the heat, warm through, then begin adding the stock, a large ladle at a time, stirring gently until each ladle has almost been absorbed by the rice. The risotto should be kept at a bare simmer throughout cooking, so don't let the rice dry out—add more stock as necessary. Continue until the rice is tender and creamy, but the grains still firm (15–20 minutes depending on the type of rice used—check the package instructions).

Season to taste with salt and pepper, and beat in the remaining butter, the Parmesan, and the chopped basil. You may like to add a little more hot stock at this stage to loosen the risotto—it should be quite wet. Cover and let rest for a couple of minutes so the risotto can relax and the cheese melt. Carefully ladle into warm bowls and cover the surface with the roasted tomatoes and any juices. Add the basil leaves and serve immediately with extra grated Parmesan cheese.

Tomato and rice soup at its best! This risotto is full of the sweet, intense flavor of tomatoes, added in three ways: passata to the stock; sun-dried tomatoes adding their caramel flavor deep in the risotto; then tiny ripe plum tomatoes, roasted to perfect sweetness. Delicious hot—but any leftovers are irresistible and so marvellous eaten straight out of the pan.

✳ tip

If a recipe requires you to skin tomatoes, make a small cut near the stalk of each one with a sharp knife, put them in a heatproof bowl, and pour over boiling water. Leave for a minute, then pour the water away and cover the tomatoes with cold water. The skins should now peel off easily.

Fresh, homemade tomato ketchup is vastly superior to store-bought varieties as it manages to capture the true flavor of tomatoes in season. This recipe calls for the tomatoes to be slow-roasted as this results in a more intense flavor, but one that is not as full-on as barbecue sauce. The sweetness of summer-ripe tomatoes is also perfectly captured in this tart, which is essentially a tomato tarte tatin. It is flavored with fresh rosemary and little capers, but you could add any combination of ingredients that takes your fancy, such as Ligurian olives, garlic, oregano, or anchovies.

roast tomato ketchup

4½ lbs. tomatoes

3 teaspoons sea salt

leaves from a small bunch of fresh thyme

2 tablespoons olive oil

1 white onion, chopped

1 teaspoon allspice berries

½ teaspoon whole cloves

½ teaspoon black peppercorns

1½ cups sugar

1 teaspoon dry mustard powder

2 cups cider vinegar

makes about 6 cups

Preheat the oven to 300°F.

Cut the tomatoes in half and arrange cut-side up in a roasting pan. Sprinkle with 2 teaspoons of the salt and all the thyme leaves and drizzle with 1 tablespoon of the oil. Roast in the preheated oven for 1½ hours.

Heat the remaining 1 tablespoon of oil in a large saucepan over medium heat, add the onion, and sauté for 10 minutes until golden.

Put the allspice, cloves, and peppercorns in a mortar and pestle and grind to a powder. Add to the onion and cook for 1 minute. Add the roasted tomatoes, sugar, mustard powder, vinegar, and remaining 1 teaspoon salt and bring to a boil. Adjust the heat to a steady low boil and cook for 30 minutes, uncovered, stirring occasionally.

Blend to a thick sauce using a food processor or handheld blender. Pour into sterilized bottles and seal (see note on page 4).

The ketchup will keep for up to 1 year if properly sealed and stored in a cool, dark place.

upside-down tomato tart

2 tablespoons light olive oil

2 teaspoons small capers, rinsed if salted

10–12 fresh rosemary needles

3 ripe tomatoes, thickly sliced

12-oz. sheet ready-rolled puff pastry, defrosted if frozen

cracked black pepper

extra virgin olive oil, for drizzling

a non-stick, heatproof skillet, 8–9 inches diameter

serves 4, as a starter

Preheat the oven to 425°F.

Put the oil, capers, and rosemary in a non-stick, heatproof skillet. Put over high heat and when the capers start to sizzle add the tomatoes, firmly pressing them down in a single layer in the skillet. Cook for 3–4 minutes to allow the tomatoes to sizzle and soften.

Place the sheet of pastry over the tomatoes, folding in the corners, being careful not to press down on the tomatoes. Transfer the skillet to the preheated oven and cook for 18–20 minutes, until the pastry is puffed and golden. Remove the skillet from the oven and let the tart rest for a couple of minutes.

Place a serving plate that is larger than the skillet upside-down on top of the skillet and quickly flip the skillet over so the tart falls onto the plate. Sprinkle with cracked black pepper and a drizzle of olive oil and cut into 4 wedges to serve.

tomato soup

1 tablespoon olive oil

a pat of butter

1 onion, peeled and finely chopped

1 garlic glove, finely chopped

12 ripe tomatoes, halved

3 cups vegetable stock

a pinch of light packed brown sugar

freshly ground black pepper

a little heavy cream (optional)

serves 4

Heat the oil and butter in a saucepan, then fry the onion and garlic until softened, but not too brown. When the onion is soft, add the tomatoes and simmer gently, stirring occasionally, until the tomatoes have turned to mush and most of the liquid has evaporated, about 20 minutes.

Add the stock, bring to a boil, reduce the heat, and simmer gently for 15 minutes.

Purée the soup with a handheld blender or in a food processor. Return to the pan, warm through, and add the sugar and pepper. If you want to make this soup really creamy, add a little cream.

tomato, mozzarella, & basil salad

2 balls of buffalo mozzarella, 5½ oz. each

2 large ripe tomatoes, roughly the same size as the balls of mozzarella

leaves from a small bunch fresh basil

½ cup extra virgin olive oil

sea salt and freshly ground black pepper

serves 4

Cut the mozzarella and tomatoes into slices about ¼ inch thick. Arrange the tomato slices on a large plate and season. Put 1 slice of mozzarella on each slice of tomato and top with a basil leaf. Tear up the remaining basil and scatter over the top. Drizzle with a generous amount of olive oil just before serving. Serve immediately at room temperature.

chile tomato jam

2 lbs. ripe tomatoes, roughly chopped

4 red bird eye chiles, roughly chopped

2 garlic cloves, peeled

1 teaspoon grated fresh ginger

2 tablespoons light soy sauce

1 cup grated palm sugar

⅓ cup of white wine vinegar

½ teaspoon of sea salt

makes 1¼ cups

Put the tomatoes, chiles, and garlic in a food processor and process until quite smooth. Transfer to a saucepan and add the remaining ingredients. Bring to a boil and simmer gently, stirring occasionally, for 30–40 minutes, or until thick and jam-like.

Spoon into a sterilized bottle or jar (see page 4) and let cool, then seal. Refrigerate once opened.

roasted tomatoes

1 lb. ripe cherry tomatoes

olive oil, for drizzling

2 garlic cloves, unpeeled

a sprig of fresh rosemary

serves 4

Preheat the oven to 350°F.

Put the tomatoes into a roasting pan. Drizzle over a little olive oil and the garlic and rosemary. Roast in the preheated oven for 35 minutes. When they are ready to come out of the oven they look wrinkled.

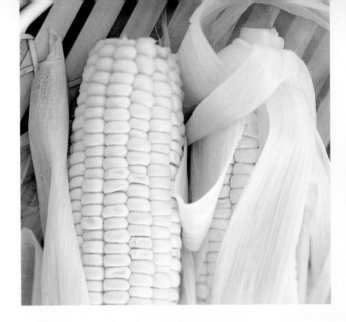

The frittata is a brilliant stand-by for a no-fuss, fast supper. Crunchy corn and asparagus work nicely here combined with farm-fresh eggs, creamy goat cheese, and fresh, tangy dill. The soup is inspired by the cuisine of America's South-west. The chile content is rather conservative, but you can spice it up as much as you like. You can also purée it for a thicker, more chowder-like consistency.

corn, asparagus, & goat cheese frittata

2 bunches of thin asparagus spears

3 tablespoons butter

kernels from 2 ears of corn (about 1½ cups)

4 scallions, finely chopped

a handful of fresh dill, chopped

8 eggs, beaten

7 oz. firm goat cheese, broken into pieces

sea salt and freshly ground black pepper

serves 4

Trim, or snap off, the woody ends from the asparagus and cut the spears into 1-inch pieces.

Heat half of the butter in a large non-stick skillet set over medium heat. Add the asparagus, corn, and scallions and fry for 2–3 minutes, stirring often. Transfer the vegetables to a large bowl and add the dill, reserving a little to use as garnish. Wipe the skillet clean. Add the beaten eggs to the vegetables, gently stirring to combine, and season well with salt and pepper.

Preheat the broiler to high. Put the remaining butter in the skillet and set over high heat. Swirl the pan around as the butter melts so that it coats the bottom and just starts to sizzle. Pour the frittata mixture into the skillet and reduce the heat to medium. Arrange the pieces of goat cheese over the top of the frittata and gently push them into the mixture. Cook for about 8 minutes, until the sides of the frittata start to puff up (reduce the heat if the bottom appears to be cooking too quickly).

Keep the frittata in the skillet and place it under the preheated broiler. Cook for 1 minute only just to set the top. Let cool a little in the skillet, sprinkle with the reserved dill, and serve immediately.

corn, zucchini, & cumin soup

3 tablespoons extra virgin olive oil

2 onions, halved, then sliced

3 zucchini (about 1½ lbs.), quartered lengthwise, then sliced

2–3 potatoes, about 10½ oz., cubed

4 garlic cloves, sliced

2 ears of corn, freshly shucked

1 teaspoon ground cumin

1 red chile, seeded and sliced

2 cups fresh unsalted chicken or vegetable stock

sea salt

to serve

crème fraîche or cream

chopped fresh cilantro

Tabasco sauce

serves 4

Heat the oil in a saucepan. Add the onions, zucchini, potatoes, and some salt and cook over high heat until beginning to brown, about 5 minutes.

Add the garlic, corn, cumin, and chile and cook, stirring, for 1 minute more. Add the stock and 1 cup water, then add salt to taste. Bring to a boil, then lower the heat and simmer gently until the potatoes are tender, 15–20 minutes. Set aside for at least 30 minutes for the flavors to develop.

To serve, reheat the soup. Ladle into soup bowls and top each with a spoonful of crème fraîche, cilantro, and a dash of Tabasco. Serve immediately.

Note For a light meal, put some flour tortillas on a baking sheet, top with grated Cheddar cheese, and toast in a hot oven until melted. Cut into wedges to serve.

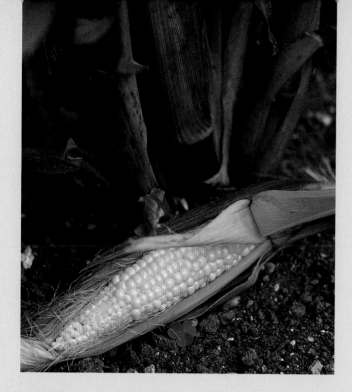

grilled corn
with chile lime butter

12 ears of corn, husked

1 stick unsalted butter, melted

a large pinch of chili powder

sea salt and freshly ground
black pepper

chile lime butter

1 teaspoon sweet chile sauce

finely grated zest and freshly
squeezed juice of 2 limes

1 stick unsalted butter,
softened

serves 6

To make the chile lime butter, put the chile, lime zest, and butter in
a bowl and beat well. Season with salt and pepper, then roll into a
cylinder between sheets of damp baking parchment. Twist the ends
and chill for at least 1 hour until hard.

To grill the corn, melt the butter in a small saucepan and whisk in
the chile and lime juice. This will be the basting sauce
for the corn.

Preheat an outdoor grill or broiler, add the corn
and cook for at least 10 minutes, basting and
turning until golden brown all over, soft, and lightly
charred. Slice the chilled butter into disks and
serve with the hot grilled corn.

Messy and meltingly delicious, grilled corn will be
a favorite with a hungry crowd. Serve with lots of
paper napkins—this is definitely a hands-on dish!
And if you have the grill already lit, cornbread
is a perfect side dish to grilled food. As it doesn't
involve yeast, cornbread is a wonderfully easy bread
to make at home, ideal to whip up when you want
fresh bread, hot from the oven. It is best made in
a heavy, cast-iron cooking dish or skillet to achieve
a crisp outer crust.

corn & sun-dried
tomato corn bread

2 tablespoons olive oil

½ cup coarse yellow cornmeal

1 cup all-purpose flour

1 teaspoon baking powder

1 tablespoon rosemary needles

½ teaspoon sea salt

1 egg

1 cup buttermilk

1 cup milk

1 cup corn kernels, fresh,
frozen, or canned

½ cup sun-dried tomatoes,
chopped

*a heavy baking dish, 11 inches
diameter, preferably cast-iron*

serves 6

Preheat the oven to 400°F.

Coat the bottom and sides of the baking dish with the oil. Put in
the preheated oven to heat up for 5 minutes.

Combine the cornmeal, flour, baking powder, rosemary, and salt in
a bowl. Beat together the egg, buttermilk, and milk, then carefully
fold it into the flour mixture along with the corn kernels and
sun-dried tomatoes.

Remove the baking dish from the oven and pour in the batter. Bake
for 30 minutes until set and golden. Let cool on a wire rack.

Slice into wedges to serve. The bread is best eaten while still warm.

You can make this hearty country tagine with fresh or tinned artichokes. If using fresh, see the tip box below on preparing them before you start. Baby artichokes are quite different from the fat, globe ones. They are slightly smaller than the size of your hand, elongated, purple-green, and usually sold in bunches. They have very immature chokes inside, which can be eaten. Try them simply pan-fried and paired with a delicious cool ricotta and thyme sauce.

tagine of artichokes, potatoes, & peas

2–3 tablespoons olive oil

2 red onions, halved lengthwise, cut in half crosswise, and sliced with the grain

4 garlic cloves, crushed

2 teaspoons coriander seeds

1 teaspoon cumin seeds

2 teaspoons ground turmeric

1–2 teaspoons dried mint

8 medium waxy potatoes, peeled and quartered

1½ cups vegetable stock

4 prepared artichokes, quartered

leaves from a small bunch of fresh cilantro, chopped

1½ cups shelled fresh peas or frozen peas

½ preserved lemon, finely shredded

sea salt and freshly ground black pepper

leaves from a small bunch of fresh mint, to serve

crusty bread or couscous, to serve

serves 4–6

Heat the olive oil in a tagine or heavy-based casserole. Add the onion and sauté, stirring, until it begins to soften. Add the garlic, coriander and cumin seeds, ground turmeric, and the dried mint. Toss in the potatoes, coating them in the spices. Pour in the stock and bring to a boil. Reduce the heat, cover, and cook gently for about 10 minutes.

Toss in the artichokes and fresh cilantro and cook for a further 5 minutes. Stir in the peas and preserved lemon, and season to taste with salt and pepper. Cook gently for 5–10 minutes, uncovered, until the artichokes are tender and the liquid has reduced.

Sprinkle with mint leaves and serve with crusty bread or couscous.

* tip

To prepare artichokes, you must first remove the outer leaves, then cut off the stems and scoop out the choke and hairy bits with a teaspoon. Rub the artichokes with lemon juice or place in a bowl of cold water with lemon juice to prevent discoloration.

pan-fried artichokes
with thyme & ricotta

8–12 medium purple-green young artichokes with stems and heads, about 4 inches long, or 12 whole char-grilled deli artichokes in oil, drained

1½ lemons

1 cup good olive oil

1–2 tablespoons freshly chopped thyme

½ cup dry white wine

at least 4½ oz. fresh ricotta cheese

sea salt and freshly ground black pepper

serves 4

To prepare the artichokes, fill a large bowl with water and squeeze in the juice of ½ lemon. Use another ½ lemon to rub the cut portions of the artichoke as you work. Snap off the dark outer leaves, starting at the base. Trim the stalk down to about 2 inches. Trim away the dark green outer layer at the base and peel the fibrous outside of the stalk with a vegetable peeler. Cut about ½ inch off the tip of each artichoke. As they are prepared, put the artichokes in the lemony water until needed. When ready to cook, drain and cut in half lengthwise.

Heat the oil in a large skillet until hot, then add the artichokes. Fry for 3 minutes without moving them, then turn them over and cook for another 2–3 minutes until tender. If using store-bought char-grilled artichokes, cut them in half and reheat gently in the olive oil for 3–4 minutes. Transfer to a warm serving dish.

Add the thyme to the skillet and cook over high heat for a few seconds to release the aroma. Add the wine and boil hard to reduce by half. Season with a squeeze of lemon juice, salt, and pepper. Crumble the ricotta around the edge of the plate, pour the hot thyme sauce on top, and serve immediately.

podding vegetables

spring vegetable pasta with lemon

pea & mint soup ❧ pea & parma ham crostini

fresh pea, tomato, & paneer curry

green couscous with a spring broth

french bean, pea, & new potato salad

fava bean, zucchini, & lemon soup

bean & chickpea salad ❧ green beans with

a spanish dressing ❧ florentine green beans

french beans with garlic

This pasta dish is admittedly more vegetable than pasta, but it's one of the most delicious ways to enjoy the new season's produce. You can vary the vegetables depending on what's available. Baby zucchini also work well, as does fennel. The key thing is to cook them until they're only just done to preserve their delicate flavor and bright green color. Pea soup is another great way to enjoy sweet spring peas—and teamed with mint it is a classic combination.

spring vegetable pasta with lemon

a small bunch of asparagus

1 cup shelled fresh peas

a few stalks of sprouting broccoli

5 oz. fava beans

1 stick butter

1 leek or ½ bunch of scallions, thinly sliced

1¼ cups heavy cream

10 oz. dried egg pasta shapes, such as Campanelle

freshly squeezed juice of 2–3 lemons (about ½ cup)

3 heaping tablespoons finely chopped fresh parsley

2 heaping tablespoons each finely chopped fresh dill and chives

sea salt and freshly ground black pepper

freshly shaved Parmesan cheese or grana padano, to serve

serves 6

Snap the asparagus spears two-thirds down the stalks and discard the woody ends. Cut the remaining stem into short lengths. Steam or microwave them for about 2–3 minutes until just cooked and refresh with cold water. Repeat with the other vegetables—steaming them individually until just cooked. (Pop the fava beans out of their skins for an even sweeter taste).

Gently melt the butter in a large saucepan or flameproof casserole and cook the leek for a couple of minutes until starting to soften. Tip in the other vegetables, lightly toss with the butter, cover the pan, and leave over very low heat, adding the cream once the vegetables have heated through.

Cook the pasta following the instructions on the packet. Reserve a little of the cooking water and drain well. Tip the drained pasta into the vegetables and toss together. Add the lemon juice and herbs, season with salt and pepper, and toss together lightly. Check the seasoning, adding extra salt, pepper, lemon juice, or a little of the reserved pasta cooking water to lighten the sauce if you think it needs it. Serve in warm bowls with shavings of Parmesan.

pea & mint soup

4 tablespoons butter

2 leeks, trimmed, split, well washed, then chopped

1 large baking potato (about 8 oz.), chopped

1 garlic clove, crushed

1½ lbs. frozen peas

1 quart chicken or vegetable stock

2 sprigs of fresh mint

2 tablespoons freshly chopped mint

sea salt and freshly ground black pepper

sour cream or crème fraîche, to serve

serves 6

Melt the butter in a saucepan, add the leeks, potatoes, and garlic and fry for 10 minutes. Add the peas, stock, mint sprigs, and a little salt and pepper and bring to a boil. Cover and simmer for 20 minutes. Discard the mint sprigs.

Transfer the soup to a blender, add the chopped mint, then purée until very smooth. Return to the pan, season to taste, and heat through. Serve the soup topped with a spoonful of sour cream and a generous grinding of black pepper.

* tip

If you have a bumper crop of peas which you are not using straight away, remove them from their pods and freeze them until they are needed. After picking, the sugar in the peas turns to starch very quickly, which impairs their sweet flavor—freezing prevents this. To bring out the sweetness in the peas, add a pinch of sugar to the pan when boiling. Never add salt, as this will make them tough.

The new season's peas are so deliciously sweet that you want to enjoy them every which way you can. Teamed with Italian cheese and ham, puréed peas make a wonderful topping for little crostini to be served with drinks. For something more substantial, this fresh-tasting, summery curry is sure to delight guests. Southern Indian food tends to have a greater emphasis on fresh ingredients, with just one or two spices thrown in. Paneer is a firm, white cheese from India—if you can't find it, halloumi works well too.

pea & parma ham crostini

ciabatta toasts

1 ready-to-bake ciabatta loaf

olive oil spray or 4–6 tablespoons light olive oil

topping

2 cups shelled fresh or frozen peas

2 scallions

½ cup finely grated aged pecorino or Parmesan cheese

1 tablespoon finely chopped fresh mint or dill

2 tablespoons fruity olive oil

4 oz. thinly sliced Parma ham or other air-dried ham, torn or cut in half

salt and freshly ground black pepper

freshly squeezed lemon juice, to taste

makes 18 crostini

To make the ciabatta toasts, preheat the oven to 350°F. Cut the ciabatta on the slant into fairly thin slices. Spray both sides with olive oil or pour olive oil in the baking sheet and dip the slices of ciabatta in it. Bake for 15 minutes, turning the slices halfway through. Remove from the oven and let cool.

For the topping, cook the peas in boiling water for 2–3 minutes or until just tender. Drain under cold running water. Trim and cut the scallions in half lengthwise, then slice very thinly.

Put the peas and onions in a food processor and pulse until you get a chunky spread. Add the pecorino and mint and pulse again, then stir in the oil. Season to taste with salt, pepper, and lemon juice. Spread the mixture thickly on ciabatta toasts and drape with a piece of ham. Serve immediately.

fresh pea, tomato, & paneer curry

2 tablespoons vegetable oil

8 oz. paneer, cubed

1 tablespoon butter

2 onions, finely chopped

2-inch piece of fresh ginger, grated

2 green chiles, seeded and finely chopped

3 ripe tomatoes, roughly chopped

2 teaspoons white wine vinegar

1½ cups peas

½ teaspoon garam masala

a handful of fresh cilantro leaves

sea salt and freshly ground black pepper

to serve

cooked basmati rice

naan bread

mango chutney

serves 4

Heat the oil in a skillet set over medium heat. Add the paneer and cook for 4–5 minutes, turning often, until golden all over. Remove from the skillet and set aside.

Add the butter to the skillet. When it is melted and sizzling, add the onions and stir-fry until softened and lightly golden. Add the ginger and chiles to the pan and cook for 1 minute.

Add the tomatoes, vinegar, and ¼ cup water and bring to a boil. Cook for about 5 minutes, to thicken slightly. Add the peas and return the paneer to the pan. Reduce the heat and simmer for about 4 minutes, until the peas are tender.

Stir in the garam masala and season to taste with salt and pepper. Sprinkle with the cilantro leaves and serve with basmati rice and an assortment of Indian accompaniments.

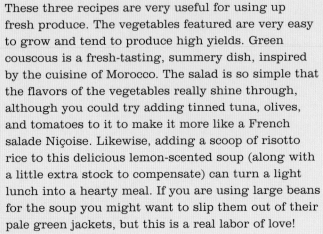

These three recipes are very useful for using up fresh produce. The vegetables featured are very easy to grow and tend to produce high yields. Green couscous is a fresh-tasting, summery dish, inspired by the cuisine of Morocco. The salad is so simple that the flavors of the vegetables really shine through, although you could try adding tinned tuna, olives, and tomatoes to it to make it more like a French salade Niçoise. Likewise, adding a scoop of risotto rice to this delicious lemon-scented soup (along with a little extra stock to compensate) can turn a light lunch into a hearty meal. If you are using large beans for the soup you might want to slip them out of their pale green jackets, but this is a real labor of love!

green couscous with a spring broth

3 cups couscous

½ teaspoon sea salt

2¾ cups warm water

1–2 tablespoons olive oil

1 tablespoon butter, broken into small pieces

4 cups vegetable or chicken stock

12 oz. fresh fava beans, shelled

6 oz. fresh or frozen peas

12 scallions, trimmed and thickly sliced

6 baby zucchini, thickly sliced

4–6 globe artichoke hearts, cut into quarters

leaves from a bunch of fresh flatleaf parsley, finely chopped

leaves from a bunch of fresh cilantro, finely chopped

leaves from a bunch of fresh mint, finely chopped

sea salt and freshly ground black pepper

serves 4–6

Preheat the oven to 400°F.

Tip the couscous into an ovenproof dish. Stir the salt into the water and pour it over the couscous. Leave the couscous to absorb the water for about 10 minutes.

Using your fingers, rub the oil into the couscous grains to break up the lumps and aerate them. Scatter the butter over the surface and cover with a piece of foil. Put in the preheated oven for about 15 minutes, until the couscous is heated through.

Meanwhile, prepare the vegetable broth. Pour the stock into a heavy-based saucepan and bring it to a boil. Add the fava beans, peas, scallions, zucchini, and artichokes and cook for 5–10 minutes, until tender. Season the broth to taste with salt and pepper and stir in the herbs.

Remove the couscous from the oven and tip it onto a serving plate. Using a slotted spoon, lift the vegetables out of the broth and arrange them around, or over, the mound of couscous. Moisten with a little of the broth, then pour the rest into a pitcher and serve separately to pour over the couscous. Serve immediately.

french bean, pea & new potato salad

1 lb. new potatoes, washed and halved, if large

a couple of sprigs of fresh mint

4 eggs

4 handfuls of fresh, shelled peas

about 7 oz. French beans, trimmed

a few handfuls of lettuce leaves

2 tablespoons olive oil

2 teaspoons red wine or cider vinegar

serves 4

Boil the new potatoes in a pan with the sprigs of mint.

Heat a pan of water over medium high heat and bring to a boil. Add the eggs and hard-boil—this should take around 7 minutes. Transfer the pan to the sink and run cold water over the eggs to cool them down. When the eggs are cool, peel off their shells and cut them into quarters.

Boil the peas and French beans. Put in a big salad bowl with the potatoes, eggs, and lettuce.

Mix together the olive oil and vinegar, add to the salad and gently mix together.

fava bean, zucchini, & lemon soup

2 tablespoons extra virgin olive oil

1 unwaxed lemon

1 onion, chopped

3 tablespoons freshly chopped flatleaf parsley, plus extra to serve

1 lb. zucchini, sliced

10 oz. fava beans (shelled weight)

3¼ cups vegetable stock

sea salt and freshly ground black pepper

lemon & thyme oil

2 unwaxed lemons

2 fresh thyme or lemon thyme sprigs

1 cup extra virgin olive oil

serves 4

To make the lemon and thyme oil, peel off the lemon zest using a peeler, leaving behind the bitter white pith. Put the zest, thyme, and olive oil in a saucepan and heat gently for 10 minutes. Remove from the heat and leave to cool. Season to taste.

For the soup, heat the oil in a large saucepan. Peel the zest from the lemon in one large piece so it's easy to find later and add that to the pan. Add the onion, parsley, and zucchini, cover, and cook over low heat, stirring occasionally, for 8 minutes or until softening. Remove the lemon zest. Add the beans and stock, season well and return to the heat for a further 20 minutes.

Transfer a quarter of the soup to a blender, liquidize until smooth, then stir back into the soup. Check the seasoning and add lemon juice to taste.

Divide the soup between 4 bowls, drizzle with some lemon and thyme oil, and serve with extra parsley and a grinding of pepper.

The rest of the lemon and thyme oil can be kept in a sealed jar in the refrigerator for up to 3 days.

bean & chickpea salad

1 lb. green beans

2 tablespoons sake or dry sherry

3 teaspoons sugar

5 teaspoons soy sauce

1 cup vegetable stock

2 tablespoons sesame seeds

14-oz. can chickpeas, drained

½ teaspoon sesame oil

serves 4

Bring a saucepan of water to a boil, add the beans, and cook for 5 minutes until tender but still firm to the bite. Drain and rinse in cold water, then plunge into iced water to set their color.

Bring the sake to the boil in a small saucepan and then transfer to a bowl and combine with the sugar and soy sauce.

Put the stock in a saucepan with 1 tablespoon of the sake mixture. Bring to a boil. Drain the beans and add to the stock. Return to a boil, then remove from the heat, drain, and leave to cool.

Heat a skillet, add the sesame seeds, and toast, keeping them moving, until they are golden. Transfer the seeds to a mortar and pestle or mini food processor and grind them to a rough paste.

In a bowl, combine the ground sesame seeds with the chickpeas, oil, and the remaining sake mixture, then toss through the drained beans. Serve immediately.

green beans with a spanish dressing

1 pink banana shallot or 2 large shallots, chopped

2 tablespoons white wine vinegar

1 garlic clove

a pinch of sugar

4 tablespoons extra virgin olive oil

14 oz. thin green beans

1 hard-boiled egg, finely chopped

1 tablespoon freshly chopped flat leaf parsley

sea salt and freshly ground black pepper

serves 6–8

Put the chopped shallot in a small bowl and add 1 tablespoon of the vinegar and 1 tablespoon water.

Crush the garlic to a paste with the sugar and a pinch of salt. Add pepper and the remaining vinegar and gradually whisk in the oil to make a dressing.

Cook the beans in a saucepan of boiling salted water for about 4 minutes until just cooked but still crisp. Drain and transfer to a serving dish. Pour over the dressing and mix well. Rinse and drain the shallot. Sprinkle the shallot, egg, and parsley on top of the beans and serve warm or cold.

florentine green beans

1½ lbs. beans, topped and tailed

4 tablespoons extra virgin olive oil

1 medium onion, thinly sliced

1 teaspoon fennel seeds, lightly crushed

1 tablespoon tomato paste

1 scant cup warm water

sea salt and freshly ground black pepper

serves 4

Bring a saucepan of salted water to a boil and add the beans. Boil for about 6 minutes until tender yet crisp. Meanwhile, heat the oil in a skillet and cook the onion for about 5 minutes until just beginning to color and soften. Drain the beans as soon as they are cooked and set aside.

Add the crushed fennel seeds to the onion with plenty of salt and pepper. Mix the tomato paste with the warm water and add to the onion mixture. Bring to a boil and stir in the beans, tossing well to coat with the sauce. Taste and season again. Cover and simmer gently for 5 minutes more, then serve.

french beans with garlic

1½ lbs. French beans, trimmed

2 tablespoons olive oil

1 tablespoon unsalted butter

2 garlic cloves, crushed

a handful of fresh flatleaf parsley, chopped

1 teaspoon freshly squeezed lemon juice

sea salt and freshly ground black pepper

serves 4

Bring a large saucepan of water to a boil. Add the beans and cook for 3–4 minutes from the time the water returns to a boil. Drain and refresh under cold running water. Set aside.

Heat the olive oil and butter in a skillet. Add the garlic, the beans, and a little salt, and cook on high for 1 minute, stirring. Remove from the heat and stir in the parsley and lemon juice. Sprinkle with black pepper and serve.

greens & salad vegetables

cauliflower & swiss chard salad

cauliflower gratin ❧ **cauliflower masala**

creamy cauliflower & gruyère soup

spaghetti with broccoli, walnuts, & ricotta

tenderstem broccoli, shiitake, & tofu omelette

braised red cabbage with chestnuts & apples

red cabbage & currant pickle ❧ **cabbage, sprouts,**

& lettuce sauté ❧ savoy cabbage with bacon & cream

punjabi cabbage ❧ creamy coleslaw

baked spinach mornay ❧ fresh spinach & chickpea curry

sautéed spinach with orange & almonds

spinach & cheese burek ❧ **swiss chard, feta cheese,**

& egg pie ❧ swiss chard & brown lentil soup

chilled lettuce soup ❧ caesar salad

rocket & fennel salsa verde

The distinctive thick leaves that seem to hug the head of a cauliflower are actually protecting the white "flower" from the sun. In doing so, they deprive it of what it needs to turn green, and that's essentially the difference between the cauliflower and its close relative broccoli. Cauliflower is often overlooked in favor of other brassicas, such as broccoli, that are quicker to cook. But it has an intense flavor which works so well in this light and spicy Middle Eastern-style salad, and also with creamy cheeses such as in this gratin.

cauliflower & swiss chard salad

¼ cup light olive oil

1 small head of cauliflower, separated into large florets

1 teaspoon ground cumin

6 large Swiss chard leaves, chopped into 1-inch wide strips

1 red onion, cut into wedges

2 garlic cloves, chopped

14-oz. can chickpeas, rinsed and drained

¼ cup tahini (sesame seed paste)

2 tablespoons freshly squeezed lemon juice

¼ teaspoon freshly cracked white pepper

sea salt

serves 4

Put the oil in a skillet set over high heat, add the cauliflower florets, and cook for 8–10 minutes, turning often, until they are a dark, golden brown. Add the cumin and cook, stirring, for 1 minute. Add the Swiss chard, onion, and garlic to the skillet and cook for a further 2–3 minutes. Add the chickpeas and stir. Season to taste with salt.

Combine the tahini, lemon juice, and white pepper in a small bowl and add a little salt to taste. Whisk to combine. Transfer the vegetables to a bowl and drizzle the dressing over the top to serve.

✳ tip

The secret of delicious cauliflower is to blanch it first; if you parboil it with a bay leaf, the unpleasant cabbage aroma disappears completely.

cauliflower gratin

1 fresh bay leaf

1 large cauliflower, separated into large florets

2 cups heavy cream

1 egg

2 teaspoons Dijon mustard

1½ cups (about 6 oz.) grated Comté cheese*

coarse sea salt

a baking dish, about 10 inches diameter, greased with butter

serves 4–6

Bring a large saucepan of water to a boil, add the bay leaf, salt generously, then add the cauliflower florets. Cook for about 10 minutes, until still slightly firm. Drain and set aside.

Put the cream in a saucepan and bring to a boil. Boil for 10 minutes. Add a spoonful of hot milk to the beaten egg to warm it, then stir the egg, mustard, and 1 teaspoon salt into the cream.

Preheat the oven to 400°F. Divide the cauliflower into smaller florets, then stir them into the cream sauce. Transfer to the prepared baking dish and sprinkle the cheese over the top in an even layer. Bake in the preheated oven for 40–45 minutes, until golden. Serve hot.

*Note Like Gruyère, Comté is a mountain cheese—from the Franche-Comté region to be precise—but the similarity stops there. Comté's distinct flavor comes from the milk used in the making, so the flavor varies with the seasons. A springtime diet of tender young shoots delivers milk that is very different from its winter counterpart, nourished mainly on hay: it is darker in color and fruitier in summer, paler and more nutty in winter. Use Emmental or Cantal if it is unavailable.

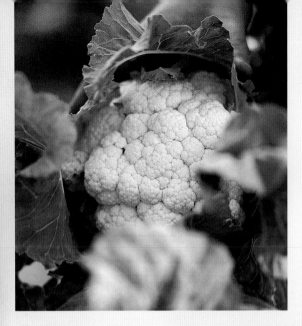

Cauliflower makes a substantial meal in itself and these two simple suppers are perfect if you have plenty of produce but not much else in the pantry! In this simple masala, cauliflower florets are stir-fried in a seasoned, spiced oil until just tender. Substitute broccoli florets if desired, to ring the changes. A small, whole head of cauliflower that is creamy-white and soft is best for this soup as the recipe does not involve straining the puréed mixture. Although this dish is somewhere between being a soup and a fondue, it knows exactly what it is— deliciously creamy and cheesy.

cauliflower masala

1 tablespoon safflower oil

2 teaspoons cumin seeds

1 teaspoon black mustard seeds

1 lb. cauliflower florets

2 garlic cloves, thinly sliced

2 teaspoons finely chopped fresh ginger

1 green chile, thinly sliced

1 teaspoon garam masala

⅔ cup hot water

freshly squeezed juice of ½ lemon

sea salt and freshly ground black pepper

serves 4

Heat the safflower oil in a large skillet over medium heat. Add the cumin seeds and mustard seeds. Stir-fry for 30 seconds, then add the cauliflower, garlic, ginger, and chile. Turn the heat to high and stir-fry for 6–8 minutes, or until the cauliflower is lightly browned at the edges.

Stir in the garam masala and hot water and stir well. Cover and cook over high heat for 1–2 minutes.

Season well and drizzle with the lemon juice just before serving.

creamy cauliflower & gruyère soup

2 tablespoons butter

1 onion, roughly chopped

1 celery stick, chopped

1 small cauliflower (about 2 lbs.), cut into small pieces

1½ quarts vegetable or chicken stock

1 cup heavy cream

2 cups grated Gruyère cheese, plus extra to serve

sea salt and freshly ground black pepper

freshly chopped parsley and toasted wholemeal bread, to serve

serves 4

Heat the butter in a saucepan over high heat. Add the onion and celery and cook for 5 minutes, until the onion has softened but not browned.

Add the cauliflower pieces and stock and bring to a boil. Allow to boil for 25–30 minutes, until the cauliflower is really soft and breaking up in the stock.

Transfer the mixture to a food processor or blender and process the mixture in batches until smooth. Return the purée to a clean saucepan. Add the cream and cheese and cook over low heat, stirring constantly, until the cheese has all smoothly melted into the soup.

Season to taste with a little sea salt and black pepper. Serve sprinkled with chopped parsley and extra cheese and with buttered wholemeal toast on the side.

Broccoli is a relatively modern vegetable. It was developed in Italy from the now trendy purple sprouting broccoli. There is actually very little to choose between them in taste so it's just a question of whether you prefer the compactness of a head or the leafiness of the sprouting variety. They both get a role in these two perfect midweek-supper dishes. The light texture and creamy flavor of ricotta cheese makes the perfect backdrop to walnuts and broccoli in this deliciously simple and quick pasta dish. The omelet has a distinctly Asian feel with the creamy cubes of tofu replacing the more traditional cheese.

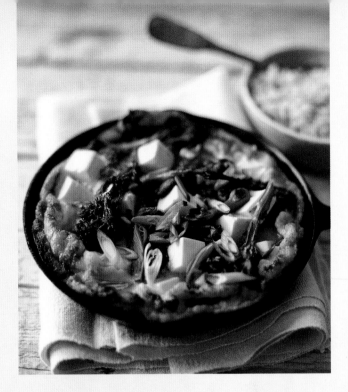

spaghetti with broccoli, walnuts, & ricotta

⅔ cup walnut halves

1 head of broccoli (about 1 lb.)

3 tablespoons light olive oil

3 garlic cloves, thinly sliced

a handful of fresh flatleaf parsley, chopped

finely grated zest and freshly squeezed juice of 1 unwaxed lemon

7 oz. fresh ricotta cheese

14 oz. spaghetti

sea salt and freshly ground black pepper

serves 4

Preheat the oven to 350°F. Spread the walnuts out on a baking sheet and roast in the preheated oven for about 8 minutes, shaking the sheet occasionally, until they start to brown.

To prepare the broccoli, trim off the gnarly part, about 1 inch from the stem end, and discard. Thinly slice the stem until you reach the point where it starts to branch into florets. Slice off the individual florets. Heat the oil in a skillet, add the stems, and cook for about 2–3 minutes, turning often, then add the florets and cook for about 5 minutes, until the broccoli has softened. Add the garlic, parsley, lemon zest, and walnuts and cook for 5 minutes, stirring often. Reduce the heat to medium and stir through the ricotta and lemon juice. Season well with salt and pepper and leave in the skillet to keep warm.

Cook the spaghetti according to the packet instructions. Drain and return it to the warm pan with the sauce. Stir gently to combine and serve immediately.

tenderstem broccoli, shiitake, & tofu omelet

1 tablespoon light olive oil

2 shallots, sliced

1 bunch of tenderstem broccoli, chopped into small pieces

7 oz. shiitake mushrooms

1 cup baby spinach leaves

2 teaspoons light soy sauce

10 oz. firm tofu, cubed

8 eggs, lightly beaten

ground white pepper

oyster sauce, to serve (optional)

serves 4

Put the oil in a large, non-stick skillet and set over high heat. Add the shallots, broccoli, and mushrooms and stir-fry for 3–4 minutes, until the mushrooms are soft and the broccoli turns a bright, emerald green. Add the spinach and cook until just wilted. Add the soy sauce and stir. Arrange the cubes of tofu over the vegetables so that they are evenly spaced. Preheat the broiler to high. Pour the beaten eggs into the pan and cook over high heat until the edges have puffed up.

Keep the omelet in the skillet, place it under the preheated broiler, and cook until golden and firm on top. Remove and let cool a little before drizzling with the oyster sauce (if using), then sprinkle with white pepper to serve.

Variation Try replacing the broccoli with young, tender peas and add a sprinkling of fresh cilantro.

Red cabbage is a firm winter favorite; it is great for adding color to dishes, and goes especially well with rich meats. This instant sweet-and-sour pickle is a great quick condiment to have at the ready, especially with sausages, while braised cabbage with apples and chestnuts is a perfect side to a Sunday roast or even a Christmas goose. Serve it with the same wine as used in the cooking.

braised red cabbage with chestnuts & apples

1 red cabbage

3 tablespoons unsalted butter

1 onion, halved and thinly sliced

3 oz. bacon lardons

3 cooking apples, peeled, cored, and chopped

7 oz. vacuum-packed whole peeled chestnuts

2 teaspoons coarse sea salt

1 cup dry white wine, preferably Riesling

1 tablespoon sugar

serves 4–6

Cut the cabbage in quarters, then core and slice thinly.

Melt 2 tablespoons of the butter in a skillet. Add the onion and lardons and cook for about 3 minutes, until soft.

Add the remaining butter, the cabbage, apples, and chestnuts and stir well. Season with salt, then add the wine, sugar, and 1 cup water.

Bring to a boil, boil for 1 minute, then cover and simmer gently for about 45 minutes, until the cabbage is tender.

red cabbage & currant pickle

3 tablespoons olive oil

½ small red cabbage, thinly sliced

¼ cup red wine

3 tablespoons brown sugar

¼ cup balsamic vinegar

¼ cup currants

¼ cup pine nuts

makes about 2½ cups

Heat the oil in a large skillet over low to medium heat. Add the cabbage, cover, and cook for 5 minutes. Turn up the heat to high, add the wine, and let it bubble, then add the sugar, vinegar, and currants. Cook, stirring, for 5 minutes.

Heat a skillet to medium, add the pine nuts, and toast, stirring, until golden. Stir the toasted pine nuts into the pickle. Leave to cool and refrigerate until needed. The pickle will keep in the refrigerator for up to 2 weeks.

✳ tip

Unlike other types of cabbage, red cabbage can be braised slowly and will not spoil from prolonged cooking times. Braised cabbage also freezes very well, which is good news as 1 cabbage will produce several servings. Cook up a batch and store some in the freezer for up to 3 months.

cabbage, sprouts, & lettuce sauté

14 oz. Brussels sprouts

1 tablespoon olive oil

1 tablespoon butter

1 teaspoon caraway seeds

¼ green cabbage, thinly sliced

½ iceberg lettuce, cut into ¼-inch slices

freshly squeezed juice of ½ lemon

½ teaspoon sea salt

serves 4–6

Separate as many leaves as you can from the Brussels sprouts and then finely slice any remaining leaves that are too tight to separate. Set aside.

Heat a large sauté pan or wok. Add the oil and butter and heat to medium. Add the caraway seeds and sizzle for about 30 seconds. Add the sprouts and cabbage and stir-fry for about 4 minutes until wilted. Add the lettuce, stir-fry for a further minute, then quickly transfer to a serving dish to stop the cooking. Pour over the lemon juice and sprinkle with the salt. Toss and serve immediately.

savoy cabbage with bacon & cream

1 bay leaf

1 savoy cabbage

2 tablespoons butter

1 tablespoon extra virgin olive oil

3½ oz. thinly sliced pancetta, chopped

a sprig of fresh sage, leaves stripped and thinly sliced

4 tablespoons heavy cream or crème fraîche

sea salt and freshly ground black pepper

serves 4

Bring a large saucepan of water to a boil with a bay leaf and a large pinch of salt. Quarter the cabbage and blanch in the boiling water for 2–3 minutes. Drain well.

Core the cabbage quarters, then slice crosswise.

Heat the butter and olive oil in a large skillet. Add the pancetta and sage and cook over high heat, stirring often, for 1 minute. Add the cabbage and a pinch of salt and cook, stirring often, for 2–3 minutes.

Stir in the cream and cook until warmed through, about 1 minute. Season generously with pepper and mix well. Add salt and pepper to taste and serve hot.

punjabi cabbage

3 tablespoons safflower oil

4 shallots, finely chopped

2 teaspoons finely grated fresh ginger

2 teaspoons crushed garlic

2 green chiles, halved lengthwise

2 teaspoons cumin seeds

1 teaspoon ground turmeric

1 teaspoon coriander seeds, crushed

1 lb. green or white cabbage, shredded

1 tablespoon mild or medium curry powder

1 tablespoon ghee or butter

salt and freshly ground black pepper

serves 4

Heat the safflower oil in a large, non-stick wok or skillet over low heat. Add the shallots, ginger, garlic, and chiles and stir-fry for 2–3 minutes, or until the shallots have softened.

Add the cumin seeds, turmeric, and coriander seeds and stir-fry for 1 minute.

Turn the heat to high and add the cabbage, tossing well to coat in the spice mixture. Add the curry powder and season well. Cover and cook over medium heat for 10 minutes, stirring occasionally. Stir in the ghee and serve.

creamy coleslaw

8 oz. white cabbage, shredded

6 oz. carrots, grated

½ white onion, thinly sliced

1 teaspoon salt

2 teaspoons sugar

1 tablespoon white wine vinegar

¼ cup mayonnaise

2 tablespoons heavy cream

1 tablespoon wholegrain mustard

sea salt and freshly ground black pepper

serves 4

Put the cabbage, carrots, and onion in a colander and sprinkle with the salt, sugar, and vinegar. Stir well and let drain over a bowl for 30 minutes.

Squeeze out excess liquid from the vegetables and put them in a large bowl. Put the mayonnaise, cream, and mustard in a separate bowl and mix well, then stir into the cabbage mixture. Season to taste with salt and pepper and serve. Store in the refrigerator for up to 3 days.

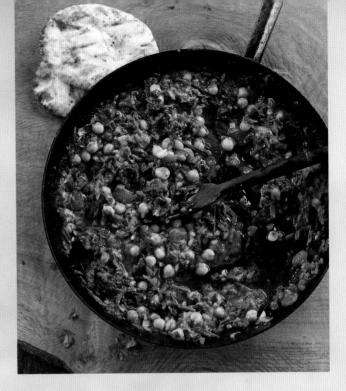

These two deliciously rich dishes prove that spinach is not about dieting or abstinence! The spinach mornay is wonderful for entertaining, ideally served with bread, to soak up the rich sauce, or a simple green salad with a tangy vinaigrette. Also great for guests is this vibrantly-colored, aromatic curry. Chickpeas are popular in India and work brilliantly here in this dish.

baked spinach mornay

3 tablespoons butter

2 tablespoons plain flour

3 cups whole milk

7 oz. Fontina cheese, cubed

1 onion, chopped

1 garlic clove, chopped

2 lbs. fresh spinach leaves, chopped

¼ teaspoon freshly grated nutmeg

toasted and buttered sourdough bread, to serve (optional)

serves 6

Preheat oven to 350°F.

Put 2 tablespoons of the butter in a saucepan set over medium heat. When it is melted and sizzling, add the flour and cook for 1 minute, stirring constantly, until a thick paste forms.

Reduce the heat to low and slowly pour the milk into the pan, whisking constantly, until all the milk is incorporated and the mixture is smooth and lump-free. Add the cheese and stir until it has melted into the sauce. Set aside until needed.

Heat the remaining butter in a large skillet set over high heat, add the onion and garlic, and cook for 2–3 minutes, until the onion has softened. Add the spinach, cover with a lid, and cook for 4–5 minutes, stirring often, until the spinach has wilted. Transfer the spinach to a large bowl. Pour in the cheese sauce and stir to combine. Spoon the mixture into a large baking dish.

Sprinkle the nutmeg over the top and bake in the preheated oven for 30 minutes until the top of the mornay is golden and bubbling. Serve on slices of toasted and buttered sourdough bread, if liked.

fresh spinach & chickpea curry

1 white onion, roughly chopped

2 garlic cloves, sliced

1 teaspoon chopped fresh ginger

1 tablespoon light olive oil

2 tablespoons mild curry paste

14-oz. can chopped tomatoes

14-oz. can chickpeas, well drained and rinsed

1 lb. fresh spinach, stalks removed and leaves chopped

a handful of fresh cilantro leaves, chopped

naan or roti bread, to serve

serves 4

Put the onion, garlic, and ginger in a food processor and process until finely chopped. Heat the oil in a skillet set over high heat. Add the onion mixture and cook for 4–5 minutes, stirring often, until golden. Add the curry paste and stir-fry for just 2 minutes, until aromatic.

Stir in the tomatoes, 1 cup cold water, and the chickpeas. Bring to a boil, then reduce the heat to a medium simmer and cook, uncovered, for 10 minutes. Stir in the spinach and cook just until it is wilted.

Stir in the cilantro and serve with the Indian bread of your choice.

Garden-fresh spinach forms the basis of these two dishes from diverse cuisines. Sautéed with orange and almonds, this Moroccan-inspired side dish is a perfect match for aromatic tagines. While in Eastern Europe, this moreish snack of spinach and cheese enveloped in golden phyllo pastry is traditionally enjoyed with a refreshing glass of keffir, a type of drinking yogurt.

sautéed spinach with orange & almonds

1 lb. fresh spinach leaves, thoroughly rinsed and drained

2–3 tablespoons olive oil and a pat of butter

1 onion, roughly chopped

2 garlic cloves, finely chopped

freshly squeezed juice and zest of 1 orange

2 tablespoons slivered almonds, toasted

sea salt and freshly ground black pepper

serves 2–4

Put the spinach in a steamer and cook for 8–10 minutes, until soft. Tip the cooked spinach onto a wooden board and chop to a pulp. Set aside.

Heat the oil and butter in a heavy-based saucepan. Stir in the onion and garlic and cook until they begin to color. Add the spinach and mix until thoroughly combined. Add the orange juice and zest and season to taste with salt and pepper.

Tip the spinach into a serving dish, garnish with the toasted almonds, and serve immediately.

spinach & cheese burek

10 oz. fresh spinach (or 1 lb. frozen spinach, defrosted and drained)

½ cup cottage cheese

½ cup Greek yogurt

1 large egg, beaten

2 tablespoons olive oil, plus extra to brush

2 tablespoons sparkling water

½ teaspoon baking soda

1 teaspoon salt

6½ oz. large phyllo pastry sheets

an 7 x 7-inch square baking pan, greased

makes 4–6 portions

Preheat the oven to 350°F.

Blanch the spinach in a saucepan of boiling water for 30 seconds. Drain and squeeze to get rid of excess water. Chop finely, then put in a mixing bowl with the cottage cheese, yogurt, egg, oil, water, baking soda, and salt, and mix well.

Lay a phyllo sheet in the base of the baking pan, leaving the excess pastry hanging over one side of the pan. Brush with oil. Lay another sheet on top so that the overhang is on the opposite side of the pan. Spread a generous tablespoon of spinach mixture over the phyllo sheet. Lay another 2 sheets over the filling and scrunch up the excess pastry to fit the pan. Brush with oil. Spread another generous tablespoon of spinach mixture over the phyllo sheet. Lay another 2 sheets over the filling and scrunch up the excess pastry to fit the pan. Brush with oil. Keep going until you've used up the spinach mixture. You should end with a layer of filling.

Finally, fold over the overhanging pastry to cover the top of the burek and brush all over with more oil. If the top isn't entirely covered with pastry, add another sheet and brush with oil.

Bake in the preheated oven for 40 minutes until deep golden and risen. Remove from the oven and leave to cool for a few minutes. It freezes well—defrost and warm up in the oven before serving.

Using fresh, seasonal ingredients simply prepared is the secret of any good recipe. Swiss chard and brown lentils make a perfect combination for hearty soups and casseroles. Or try chard in combination with feta cheese and eggs in this rustic free-form pie, where the pastry dough is simply rolled out and turned up at the edges rather than formed in a pan.

swiss chard, feta cheese, & egg pie

3 tablespoons olive oil

1 red onion, sliced

2 garlic cloves, sliced

1 lb. Swiss chard, cut into ¾-inch pieces

4 eggs

7 oz. feta cheese, crumbled

sea salt and freshly ground black pepper

pastry

2 cups all-purpose flour

1 stick plus 2 tablespoons unsalted butter, cubed

2 egg yolks

2–3 tablespoons ice water

serves 6

To make the pastry, put the flour and butter in the bowl of a food processor and put the bowl in the freezer for 10 minutes. Pulse the ingredients a few times until just combined. With the motor of the food processor running, add the egg yolks and just enough ice water so that the mixture is on the verge of coming together. Do not overbeat, as this will make the pastry tough. Remove the dough from the bowl and use lightly floured hands to quickly form it into a ball. Wrap in plastic wrap and let rest in the fridge for 30 minutes.

Put 2 tablespoons of the oil in a skillet set over high heat, add the onion and garlic, and cook for 2 minutes, until it softens and just flavors the oil. Add the Swiss chard to the skillet and cook for about 5 minutes, stirring often, until it wilts and softens. Season well with salt and pepper, leave in the skillet, and set aside to cool.

Preheat the oven to 425°F. Roll the dough out on a sheet of lightly floured baking parchment to form a circle about 14 inches in diameter, trimming away any uneven bits. Roll the edge over to form a ½-inch border, then roll over again. Transfer the pastry circle to a baking sheet. Spoon the Swiss chard mixture over the pastry.

Put the eggs in a bowl and prick the yolks with a fork. Pour the eggs over the Swiss chard so that they are evenly distributed, then scatter the feta over the top. Drizzle the remaining oil over the pie and cook in the preheated oven for about 20 minutes, until the pastry is golden and the top of the pie is just starting to turn brown.

Let cool for 10 minutes before cutting into slices to serve.

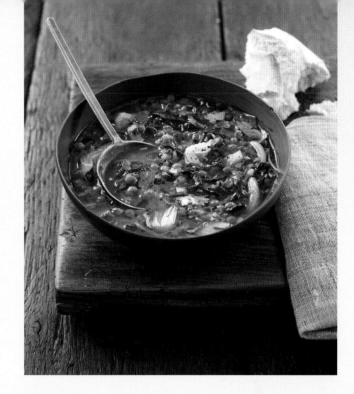

swiss chard & brown lentil soup

4 cups vegetable or chicken stock

1⅓ cups dried brown lentils

¼ cup olive oil

1 onion, chopped

4 garlic cloves, finely chopped

14 oz. Swiss chard, trimmed and thinly sliced

¼ cup freshly squeezed lemon juice

leaves from a small bunch of fresh cilantro, roughly chopped

sea salt and freshly ground black pepper

serves 4

Put the stock and lentils in a large saucepan and bring to a boil. Reduce the heat to medium and cook for 1 hour, uncovered, until the lentils are tender. Reduce the heat to low.

Heat the oil in a large skillet set over high heat. Add the onion and garlic along with a pinch of salt. Cook for 4–5 minutes, stirring often, until softened.

Stir in the chard and stir-fry for 2–3 minutes, until wilted. Add the chard mixture to the lentils and cook over low heat for 10 minutes.

Stir in the lemon juice and cilantro and season to taste with salt and pepper. Serve immediately.

Variation For a more substantial soup, add cubed chicken breast along with the Swiss chard and let it poach gently in the stock.

In the height of summer, cool, clean-tasting soups and fresh crunchy salads are a great way to start a meal. For both recipes use the freshest, just-picked lettuce, and ensure that none has bolted or is oozing a milky substance from the stem, since this may give a bitter taste. Best results are achieved if all the soup ingredients are cold before you start. This means that less chilling time is required and the lettuce will keep its crunch.

chilled lettuce soup

9 oz. lettuce, cleaned and chopped

1 cup yogurt

1 small garlic clove, crushed with a pinch of coarse salt

1-inch piece of fresh ginger, peeled and finely grated

fresh mint leaves

juice of ½ lemon

sea salt and freshly ground black pepper

serves 4

Put all the ingredients into a food processor or blender, adding just enough water to get the blades moving, and blend until the desired consistency is achieved. Blending time varies according to the type of lettuce and the type of machine you are using, but aim to make the soup fairly smooth.

caesar salad

1 romaine lettuce

⅔ cup olive oil

2 large garlic cloves, crushed

2 tablespoons freshly squeezed lemon juice, from about ½ large lemon

½ teaspoon Dijon mustard

2 anchovy fillets in oil, drained

1 large egg yolk

2 slices of stale bread, crusts removed, cubed

2 tablespoons freshly grated Parmesan cheese

sea salt and freshly ground black pepper

serves 4

Pull the leaves off the lettuce, wash them, and tear into bite-sized pieces. Spin in a salad spinner or dry on paper towels. Store in a sealed plastic bag in the refrigerator to keep it crisp.

Put 3 tablespoons olive oil in a blender or food processor and add half the garlic, the lemon juice, mustard, anchovies, and egg yolk. Blend until smooth, then transfer to a pitcher, taste, and season with salt and pepper.

Pour the remaining olive oil into a skillet, add the remaining garlic, and heat until it starts to sizzle. Scoop out the garlic, then add the cubed bread. Fry until golden, keeping the pieces on the move while they are cooking. Lift out and drain on paper towels.

Stir the dressing, pour over the salad leaves, toss well, then transfer to a bowl. Add the croutons, sprinkle with the Parmesan, and serve immediately.

Variation If anchovies don't appeal, liven up the dressing with a dash of Worcestershire sauce. You can use other kinds of salad leaves, such as radicchio, iceberg, or Chinese leaves—just remember that they must be crisp to bring out the crunchiness of the salad.

A sharp, pungent, and versatile spooning sauce, salsa verde is the perfect foil to rich foods such as ham, pork, and salmon. It is also great served with fish, lamb, chicken, potatoes, or pasta.

arugula & fennel salsa verde

2 teaspoons fennel seeds

1 garlic clove

1 tablespoon small drained capers

3 anchovy fillets

1 oz. arugula, chopped

2 tablespoons freshly chopped flatleaf parsley

1 tablespoon freshly squeezed lemon juice

4 tablespoons olive oil

sea salt and freshly ground black pepper

makes about ½ cup

Heat a skillet over medium heat and add the fennel seeds. Toast them, stirring, for about 1 minute until fragrant. Let cool. Transfer to a mortar and pestle and grind to a rough powder.

Combine the ground fennel seeds, garlic, capers, and anchovies in a small bowl and pound until blended. Alternatively, blend them in a mini food processor. Add the arugula, parsley, lemon juice, and oil and mix to combine until you have a coarse sauce. Season to taste with salt and pepper. The salsa will keep in the refrigerator for up to 1 week, but it will quickly start to discolor, so is best used when freshly made.

zucchini & squash

pumpkin soup with honey & sage

thai red pumpkin curry ❧ **roasted pumpkin wedges**

with lime & spices ❧ pumpkin & ginger jam

pumpkin & cinnamon phyllo strudel

butternut squash bread pudding with corn

roasted squash wedges with pumpkin seed pesto

spaghetti with squash, sage, & pecorino

baby squash stuffed with pine nuts & currants

sweet squash, pecan, & maple syrup tart

squash & eggplant chutney ❧ zucchini gratin with

herbs & goat cheese ❧ **zucchini & fennel tart**

grilled zucchini ❧ **zucchini sautéed with pancetta & thyme**

minted zucchini frittata ❧ **honey-roasted zucchini**

with feta ❧ chocolate & zucchini cake

zucchini, lemon thyme, & feta loaf

Pumpkin and sage are a wonderful combination and make a rich, comforting soup. Instead of fried sage leaves to garnish, you could also try sprinkling over a few toasted pumpkin seeds before serving. This recipe uses vegetable stock, but you could base it on chicken stock, too.

pumpkin soup with honey & sage

5 tablespoons unsalted butter

1 small–medium onion, roughly chopped

1 carrot, finely chopped

1 garlic clove, crushed

2¼ lbs. pumpkin or butternut squash, seeded, peeled, and cut into cubes

2 heaping tablespoons clear honey

3 sprigs of fresh sage, plus extra crisp-fried leaves (optional), to serve

3 cups vegetable stock

⅓ cup heavy cream

freshly squeezed lemon juice, to taste

sea salt and freshly ground black pepper

serves 4–6

Gently melt the butter in a large lidded saucepan or flameproof casserole. Add the onion, carrot, and garlic, stir, cover, and cook over low heat for about 4–5 minutes. Add the cubed pumpkin, honey, and sage, stir, replace the lid, and continue to cook very gently for about 10 minutes. Pour in the stock, bring to a boil and cook for a further 10 minutes until the vegetables are soft. Turn off the heat and allow the soup to cool slightly, then remove the sage and strain the soup, retaining the liquid. Put half the cooked vegetables in a food processor with just enough of the reserved cooking liquid to blend into a smooth purée.

Transfer to a clean saucepan and repeat with the remaining vegetables, adding the purée to the first batch. Whizz the remaining liquid in the food processor to pick up the last bits of purée and add that too. Bring the soup slowly to a boil, then stir in the cream without boiling further. Season to taste with lemon juice (about 1 tablespoon), salt (about a teaspoon), and pepper.

Serve with an extra swirl of cream or scatter some crisp-fried sage leaves on top and serve with whole-wheat or multigrain bread.

These are two great ways to enjoy pumpkin. Serve spicy wedges on their own or with any roasted or grilled meat or poultry dish. Save the seeds and roast them lightly with a little oil and coarse salt as a nibble, or to garnish the soup opposite. You can use butternut squash in this Thai curry instead of the pumpkin if you prefer. To elaborate on the dish for a dinner party, throw in some cooked king prawns 5 minutes before the end of the cooking time.

thai red pumpkin curry

2 tablespoons safflower oil

1 red onion, thinly sliced

2 garlic cloves, crushed

1 teaspoon finely grated fresh ginger

3 tablespoons Thai red curry paste

1¾ lbs. pumpkin flesh, cut into bite-sized pieces

1⅔ cups coconut milk

⅔ cup vegetable stock

6 kaffir lime leaves, plus extra, shredded, to garnish

2 teaspoons grated palm sugar

3 lemongrass stalks, bruised

salt and freshly ground black pepper

Thai sweet basil leaves, to garnish

serves 4

Heat the safflower oil in a large, non-stick wok or skillet. Add the onion, garlic, and ginger and stir-fry for 3–4 minutes. Stir in the curry paste and pumpkin and stir-fry for 3–4 minutes.

Add the coconut milk, stock, lime leaves, lemongrass, and palm sugar. Bring to a boil, then reduce the heat to low and simmer gently for 20–25 minutes, stirring occasionally, or until the pumpkin is tender.

Season well and garnish with the Thai basil leaves and shredded lime leaves just before serving.

roasted pumpkin wedges with lime & spices

1 medium-sized pumpkin, halved lengthwise, seeded, and cut into 6–8 segments

2 teaspoons coriander seeds

1 teaspoon cumin seeds

1 teaspoon fennel seeds

1–2 teaspoons ground cinnamon

2 dried red chiles, chopped

2 garlic cloves

2 tablespoons olive oil

coarse sea salt

finely grated zest of 1 lime

6 wooden or metal skewers, to serve (optional)

serves 6

Preheat the oven to 400°F.

Using a mortar and pestle, grind all the dried spices with the salt. Add the garlic and a little of the olive oil to form a paste. Rub the mixture over the pumpkin wedges and place them, skin-side down, in a baking dish or roasting pan. Cook them in the preheated oven for 35–40 minutes, or until tender. Sprinkle over the lime zest and serve hot, threaded onto skewers, if using.

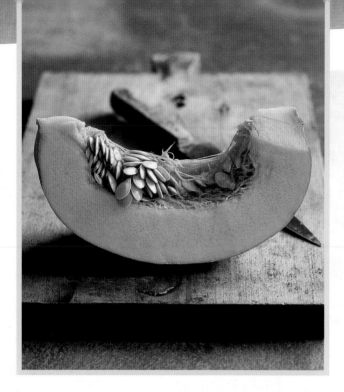

pumpkin & ginger jam

2¼ lbs. prepared pumpkin, cut into 1-inch cubes

grated zest and freshly squeezed juice of 2 large lemons

5 cups granulated sugar

3-inch piece of fresh ginger, sliced

1 lb. tart apples, peeled, cored, and chopped

2–3 oz. stem ginger in syrup, drained and cut into shreds

a small piece of cheesecloth

kitchen string

4–5 sterilized jars
(see note on page 4)

makes 4–5 small (8 oz.) jars

In a large non-reactive bowl, layer the pumpkin, lemon zest, and sugar. Wrap the fresh ginger and any lemon pips and flesh in a piece of cheesecloth tied with string and bury it in the middle of the pumpkin. Pour over the lemon juice, cover with plastic wrap, and leave in a cool place for 24 hours, stirring once.

Pour the mixture into a large preserving pan and add the apples. Tie the bag of ginger and lemon mixture to the handle of the pan so that the bag is suspended in the mixture.

Stir over low heat until the sugar completely dissolves, then increase the heat and simmer gently until the pumpkin softens. Increase the heat again and boil vigorously until setting point is reached, about 8–10 minutes*. Remove the cheesecloth bag, squeezing it against the side of the pan, then stir in the stem ginger. Let the jam cool for 15 minutes, stir to distribute the ginger, then transfer to hot, dry, sterilized jars and seal immediately.

*To test for set, see instructions on page 166.

Here are two perfect recipes for early autumn—a crumbly, heavenly phyllo strudel made with creamy, sweet pumpkin and a hint of cinnamon, and a fragrant and gloriously amber-colored preserve. Serve the jam with scones and clotted cream, as a filling for cakes or tarts, or with your toast or croissant at breakfast. This recipe makes a softly set jam, which will store well for at least 9 months, but keep in the refrigerator once opened.

pumpkin & cinnamon phyllo strudel

a small pie pumpkin, about ½ lb.

½ teaspoon ground cinnamon

¼ cup sugar

3 large sheets of thick phyllo pastry (18 x 13 inches)

1½ tablespoons vegetable oil

confectioners' sugar, to dust

a baking sheet, greased

makes 6 slices

Preheat the oven to 325°F.

Peel and seed the pumpkin, then grate the flesh and squeeze out any excess water. Put in a bowl and mix with the cinnamon and sugar.

Take one sheet of phyllo pastry, lay it on the prepared baking sheet, and lightly brush with oil. Place a second sheet on top and lightly brush with oil. Repeat with the third sheet.

Spoon the pumpkin filling along one longer side of the phyllo sheets, leaving a 1-inch gap on either side and spreading the filling about 2 inches wide. Fold the longer side of the pastry, nearest the filling, about 1 inch in, then roll the phyllo pastry up, tucking in the sides as you go. When the strudel is baking, the filling will soften and some juice might seep out, so tucking in the sides ensures that not too much juice is lost.

Brush the top of the strudel with a little more oil and bake in the preheated oven for 25 minutes. The strudel should be pale gold. Remove from the oven and leave to cool for 5 minutes. Dust liberally with confectioners' sugar and serve warm.

One of the simplest and most delicious things you can do with a winter squash is cut it into wedges and roast it. The roasting emphasizes the sweetness and chestnutty denseness of the squash and lends itself to a zesty, full-flavored pesto such as this one. For something more substantial, try a savory bread pudding—the sweetness of the squash and corn go well with the creamy, cheesy bread pudding part. In place of the baguette, you could save up the ends from sliced loaves. And any kind of cheese can be used here, as can a combination of cheeses, so it's a good way to use up odds and ends.

butternut squash bread pudding with corn

1 tablespoon olive oil

1 large onion, halved and thinly sliced

1½ cups milk

1 cup light cream

3 eggs, beaten

a small bunch of fresh chives, snipped

leaves from a small bunch of fresh parsley, finely chopped

1 baguette, cut into ¼-inch slices

2 cups corn kernels, freshly shucked, canned, or frozen

about 1 lb. peeled and sliced butternut squash

1 cup grated sharp Cheddar cheese

sea salt and freshly ground black pepper

a 12 x 8 inch baking dish, very well buttered

serves 4–6

Preheat the oven to 375°F.

Heat the oil in a large skillet. Add the onion and cook over low heat for 3–5 minutes, until soft. Season lightly and set aside.

Combine the milk, cream, and eggs in a small bowl and whisk to combine. Season with 1½ teaspoons salt. Add the chives and parsley, mix well, and set aside.

Arrange half the baguette slices in the prepared baking dish in a single layer; you may need to tear some to cover all the space. Put half of the onion slices on top, then scatter over half of the corn. Arrange half of the squash slices evenly on top and sprinkle with half of the cheese. Repeat one more time (bread, onion, corn, squash, cheese). Stir the milk mixture and pour it evenly all over the pudding.

Cover tightly with foil and bake in the preheated oven for 20 minutes. Remove the foil and continue baking for about 30–40 minutes, until golden. Serve immediately.

roasted squash wedges with pumpkin seed pesto

1 medium-sized winter squash or 2 smaller ones, such as Red Kuri or Butternut, unpeeled

extra virgin olive oil, to drizzle

a few fresh sage leaves

for the pesto

3 tablespoons pumpkin seeds

1 garlic clove

a small bunch of fresh flatleaf parsley

1 small dried red chile, crumbled, seeds discarded (optional)

1 oz. semi-dried tomatoes in olive oil, drained

¼ cup each freshly grated Parmesan cheese and pecorino cheese or ½ cup Parmesan

3–4 tablespoons extra virgin olive oil

freshly squeezed lemon juice or 1–2 tablespoons of crème fraîche, to taste

sea salt and freshly ground black pepper

serves 4

Preheat the oven to 400°F.

Cut the squash into wedges, discarding the seeds and pith as you go. Put it on a baking sheet, season, drizzle with some olive oil (about 1 tablespoon per wedge), and add a few torn sage leaves. Roast, uncovered, until tender, about 35–40 minutes, turning and basting with the oil once.

Meanwhile, make the pesto. Toast the pumpkin seeds in a dry skilletp over low heat for a few minutes. Do not allow them to burn. In a food processor, process the pumpkin seeds, garlic, parsley, chile, and tomatoes to make a rough paste. Add the cheese and then the oil, enough to make a spoonable pesto. Taste the pesto and add a squeeze of lemon juice to sharpen or crème fraîche to soften the flavor according to taste. Serve immediately with the wedges.

These two squash dishes are Italian inspired. The baby squash is packed full of Sicilian flavors, and the unexpected mix of sweet currants with the saltiness of the capers and the cheese is quite wonderful. The lemon and mint lifts the whole thing. Serve it either warm or at room temperature. This tasty pasta is inspired by the classic Italian dish of pumpkin-filled ravioli with sage butter, except this is an inside-out version and therefore much easier to make!

baby squash stuffed with pine nuts & currants

4 small acorn squashes or 4 good-sized zucchini

1 tablespoon salted capers

¼ cup currants

1 medium onion, finely chopped

5–6 tablespoons extra virgin olive oil

2–3 garlic cloves, finely chopped

1¼ cups fresh white breadcrumbs

2 tablespoons freshly chopped flatleaf parsley

2 tablespoons freshly chopped mint leaves

1–2 teaspoons grated lemon zest

½ cup freshly grated Parmesan cheese,

⅓ cup pine nuts, lightly toasted

1 egg, beaten (optional)

1 tablespoon freshly squeezed lemon juice

sea salt and freshly ground black pepper

an ovenproof baking dish, oiled

serves 4

If using acorn or other small summer squash, just cut off a thin slice from the base so that they stand upright without wobbling, then cut off a lid and scoop out the seeds to make a cavity. If using zucchini, halve them lengthwise and, using a teaspoon, remove the seeds in the centre to leave a "boat" shape. Season the cut surfaces with salt and leave them upside down to drain. In two separate bowls, cover the capers and currants with warm water and leave them to soak.

When the squashes or zucchini have drained for 45–60 minutes, rinse them, pat dry, then steam for 10–12 minutes until just tender. Drain on paper towels. Preheat the oven to 375°F.

Meanwhile, gently fry the onion in 2 tablespoons of the oil with a pinch of salt until soft and sweet, about 10–15 minutes. Add the garlic and cook for another 3–4 minutes. Drain the capers and currants. Mix the onion and garlic with all the other ingredients except the egg, remaining oil, and lemon juice. Season to taste. Stir in the egg for a firmer stuffing, if desired. Put the squash or zucchini in a baking dish and fill the cavities with the stuffing. Mix together the remaining oil and lemon juice and spoon it over the vegetables. Bake in the preheated oven for 30–35 minutes, basting once, until golden and crisp on top. Serve warm with a Greek-style salad.

spaghetti with squash, sage & pecorino

¼ cup light olive oil

14 oz. butternut squash, peeled, seeded, and cut into thin wedges

2 garlic cloves, chopped

10–12 small fresh sage leaves

14 oz. spaghetti

a handful of fresh flatleaf parsley, chopped

½ cup freshly grated pecorino cheese

sea salt and freshly ground black pepper

serves 4

Put the oil in a skillet and set over high heat. Add the squash and cook for 5–6 minutes, turning often, until golden but not breaking up. Add the garlic and sage to the pan and cook for 2–3 minutes. Remove from the heat and let sit to allow the flavors to develop.

Cook the pasta according to the packet instructions. Drain well and return to the warm pan with the squash mixture. Add the parsley and half of the pecorino and season well with salt and pepper. Serve immediately with the remaining cheese sprinkled over the top.

This tart is one of those rare recipes that tastes just as good, if not better, in reality than on the mind's palate. The squash cuts the rich toffee of the more traditional pecan pie making it softer and more tender. The maple syrup adds a subtle smokiness. You'll need a sweet, orange-fleshed squash or pumpkin here; any of the French or Italian varieties (such as Jaspée de Vendée, Sucrine du Berry, or Pleine de Naples) will work, as will Delicata squash. It's best served warm, not hot, with chilled cream or vanilla ice cream.

sweet squash, pecan, & maple syrup tart

for the pastry

1⅓ cups all-purpose flour

2 tablespoons confectioners' sugar

6 tablespoons unsalted butter, chilled

1 egg yolk

1–2 tablespoons freshly squeezed lemon juice

tart filling

2 tablespoons unsalted butter

10 oz. prepared squash or pumpkin, coarsely grated

¼ cup raw sugar

2 tablespoons bourbon or rum

⅔ cup pecan halves, half chopped

2 eggs

grated zest of 1 lemon

⅔ cup dark, pure maple syrup

½ teaspoon vanilla extract

⅔ cup heavy cream

confectioners' sugar, to dust

a deep, 8–9-inch diameter, loose-bottomed metal tart pan

serves 8

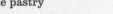

To make the pastry, put the flour, confectioners' sugar, and butter in a food processor and whizz until the mixture resembles coarse breadcrumbs. Add the egg yolk and sufficient lemon juice, a little at a time, to make a ball of dough. Wrap in foil and chill in the fridge for at least 45 minutes. Roll the dough out on a floured work surface and line the tart pan. Chill for a further 30 minutes. Preheat the oven to 375°F. Support the sides of the tart with foil and bake in the preheated oven for 12 minutes. Remove the foil, press down any air bubbles in the base and bake for another 10 minutes or until pale brown. Remove from the oven and reduce the heat to 350°F.

Meanwhile, melt the butter in a skillet and gently fry the squash for about 5 minutes until tender and lightly browned. Increase the heat a little, add 2 tablespoons of the raw sugar, and cook until it caramelizes and melts around the squash. Add the bourbon and cook briskly until a sticky syrup forms, then mix in the chopped pecans. Spoon the squash mixture into the tart crust and arrange the pecan halves on top. Beat together the eggs, remaining sugar, lemon zest, maple syrup, and vanilla extract, then gradually beat in the cream. Pour the mixture into the tart case. Bake in the still-hot oven for about 35–40 minutes, until puffed up and the centre retains a very slight wobble.

This is a golden chutney flecked with the dark purple of the eggplant and the red of the chiles. Substitute white sugar for brown for a deeper color and flavor.

squash & eggplant chutney

Put the squash and eggplant in a large, stainless steel saucepan with the onions, garlic, chiles, crushed coriander and mustard seeds, and the orange zest and juice. Bash the ginger with a rolling pin to bruise it, tie it in a piece of cheesecloth, and bury it in the mixture. Pour over the vinegar. Bring to a boil, then simmer very gently, part-covered, for 40–50 minutes until the squash is fully tender. Stir in the warmed sugar and the salt, stir until the sugar dissolves, then bring to a boil and cook briskly, stirring every few minutes, until the mixture is thick and the liquid almost all absorbed, about 30–40 minutes. Stir very frequently towards the end of cooking to prevent the mixture sticking to the base of the pan.

It is ready when a wooden spoon drawn over the base of the pan leaves a clear channel for a few seconds. Adjust the seasoning to taste with salt, cayenne, or chili powder. Leave for 10 minutes, stir well, discard the ginger, and then pot into hot, dry sterilized jars. Seal immediately, then invert. Let cool before turning the right way up. Store for at least 4 weeks before using.

Note Either use plastic-covered lids or cellophane discs to cover chutneys, as the vinegar can corrode metal. It will keep for at least 12 months in a cool, dark place. Keep in the fridge once opened.

2 lbs. prepared orange-fleshed squash or pumpkin, cubed

2 large eggplants, cubed

1½ lbs. onions, chopped

4 garlic cloves, crushed

2–3 red chiles, seeded and finely sliced or chopped (leave the seeds in if you want heat)

1 tablespoon each crushed coriander seeds and brown mustard seeds

finely shredded zest and freshly squeezed juice of 1 orange

2-oz. piece fresh ginger

1⅔ cups cider vinegar or white wine vinegar

2 cups granulated sugar, warmed

2 teaspoons salt, plus extra to taste

cayenne or chili powder, to taste

*a small piece of cheesecloth
kitchen string
4–5 sealable, sterilized jars
(see note on page 4)*

makes 4–5 medium (12 oz.) jars

zucchini gratin with herbs & goat cheese

A classic of French home cooking, this gratin includes a topping of tangy goat cheese. If you grow your own herbs, add whatever is available: savory, majoram, oregano, or any other soft-leaved herb, the more the merrier. This is perfect simply served with a mixed salad of lettuce and ripe tomatoes and a big basket of fresh crusty bread.

* tip

The zucchini has many wonderful uses—both cooked and raw (try them grated into salads), savory and sweet (they are a wonderful way to keep a sponge moist—see page 127). But what many people don't realise is that zucchini blossoms can be eaten along with the vegetable. Before they are harvested, the female flowers develop into little zucchinis; use these when the flowers are large and eat both parts. Try stuffing the flowers with soft cheese, coating them in a light batter, and frying—delicious.

1 cup heavy cream

leaves from a small bunch of fresh flatleaf parsley, finely chopped

a small bunch of fresh chives, snipped

a pinch of freshly grated nutmeg

¾ cup freshly grated Gruyère cheese

3¼ lbs. zucchini, very thinly sliced

5½ oz. soft goat cheese

sea salt and freshly ground black pepper

a 10-inch round, deep-sided baking dish, well buttered

serves 4

Preheat the oven to 375°F.

Put the cream, parsley, chives, nutmeg, salt, and pepper in a small bowl and whisk together. Add half the Gruyère.

Arrange half the zucchini slices in the prepared baking dish, sprinkle with the remaining Gruyère, and season with a little salt. Top with the remaining zucchini slices, season again, and pour over the cream mixture. Crumble the goat cheese over the top.

Bake in the preheated oven for 35–45 minutes, until browned. Serve immediately with a mixed salad and plenty of crusty bread.

Note If preferred, you can make the gratin in 4 individual dishes, simply reduce the cooking time by about 5–10 minutes.

Fresh and summery, serve this delicious zucchini and fennel tart with an arugula salad, fish, and white wine for a perfect summer picnic.

zucchini & fennel tart

1 Pizza Dough recipe (see page 56)

12 oz. zucchini, sliced ⅓ inch thick

1 small/medium fennel, trimmed and sliced ⅓ inch thick

1 small red onion, sliced ⅓ inch thick

3 tablespoons olive oil

1 teaspoon salt

½ teaspoon crushed black pepper

1 tablespoon freshly chopped parsley

¾ cup freshly grated sharp Cheddar cheese

⅔ cup Greek yogurt

a 4 x 13-inch tart pan, greased

makes about 6 portions

Preheat the oven to 400°F.

Put the zucchini, fennel, onion, oil, salt, and pepper in a roasting pan and toss until evenly combined. Cover the pan with aluminum foil. Roast in the preheated oven for 30 minutes. Remove from the oven, leave covered, and let cool for 10–15 minutes.

Reduce the oven temperature to 325°F.

Drain any excess juice from the vegetables, then mix in the parsley and about half the cheese.

Line the tart pan with the Pizza Dough but do not trim the edges yet.

Mix the yogurt and remaining cheese in a bowl, then pour into the tart crust. Scatter the roasted vegetables over the top, spreading them evenly. Bake in the hot oven for 25–30 minutes. Remove from the oven and leave to cool.

grilled zucchini

8 zucchini, cut lengthwise into ½-inch slices

olive oil

balsamic vinegar

salt and freshly ground black pepper

serves 8

Cook the zucchini slices over medium heat on a preheated outdoor grill for 3–4 minutes on each side, until lightly charred. Remove to a plate and sprinkle with oil, vinegar, salt, and pepper. Serve hot, warm, or cold.

zucchini sautéed with pancetta & thyme

1 lb. zucchini

3 tablespoons olive oil

½ cup pancetta cubes or lardons

1 tablespoon freshly chopped thyme

sea salt (optional) and freshly ground black pepper

freshly squeezed juice of ½ lemon

serves 4

Trim the zucchini and cut into cubes. Heat the oil in a skillet, add the pancetta, and fry until golden. Add the zucchini and fry over brisk heat for 3–4 minutes, tossing them around the pan from time to time until the cut sides start to turn golden.

When golden, add the thyme and plenty of black pepper (you probably won't need any salt). Season with a squeeze of lemon juice and serve immediately.

minted zucchini frittata

6 large eggs

2 tablespoons freshly chopped mint

8 oz. baby new potatoes, thickly sliced

2 tablespoons olive oil

1 large onion, chopped

4 zucchini, sliced

sea salt and freshly ground black pepper

serves 3–4

Break the eggs into a bowl and whisk briefly with a fork. Season well with salt and pepper. Mix in the chopped mint.

Cook the potatoes in a saucepan of boiling, salted water until just tender. Drain thoroughly.

Meanwhile, heat the oil in a skillet, add the onion, and cook gently for about 10 minutes, until soft and pale golden. Add the zucchini and stir over low heat for 3–4 minutes until just softened. Add the potatoes and mix gently.

Pour the eggs over the vegetables and cook over low heat until the frittata is lightly browned underneath and has almost set on top. Slide under a preheated broiler for 30–60 seconds, to set the top.

honey-roasted zucchini with feta

1 lb. zucchini, seeded if large, cut into chunky batons

2 garlic cloves, sliced

3 tablespoons extra virgin olive oil

7 oz. feta cheese, coarsely crumbled

2 tablespoons runny honey

freshly ground black pepper

a large ovenproof dish

serves 4

Preheat the oven to 425°F.

Put the zucchini into a large ovenproof dish in a single layer. Add the garlic and sprinkle with 2 tablespoons of olive oil. Using your hands, toss the zucchini batons until they are evenly coated with the garlic and oil.

Spread out the zucchini batons evenly in the dish. Scatter the feta over them and trickle with the remaining olive oil, honey, and pepper. The saltiness of the feta means that no extra salt is needed. Roast in the preheated oven until deep golden. Transfer to a serving dish and serve immediately.

If you have an excess of zucchini, they make an excellent baking ingredient—and there is a lovely retro charm, redolent of 1950s cookbooks, about making sweet cakes with a vegetable that's usually served savory. The zucchini in both these recipes performs the same function as grated carrot does in the more familiar carrot cake, keeping the sponge wonderfully moist.

chocolate & zucchini cake

2 sticks plus 1 tablespoon butter, softened

1¼ cups packed brown soft sugar

2 teaspoons vanilla extract

3 eggs

½ cup milk

2⅔ cups self-rising flour

1 teaspoon baking powder

4 tablespoons cocoa powder

1 lb. zucchini, peeled and grated

a cake pan, 12 x 8 inches, buttered and lined

makes about 20 squares

Preheat the oven to 350°F.

Put the softened butter, sugar, and vanilla extract into a bowl and beat with a wooden spoon or electric whisk until creamy.

Crack the eggs into a bowl and beat lightly with a fork. Add the eggs gradually to the bowl with the cake batter. Add the milk and whisk together.

Put a sieve over your mixing bowl and carefully pour in the flour, baking powder, and cocoa powder. Shake the sieve gently so that the ingredients snow down into the bowl. Take a metal spoon and fold into the batter. Stir in the grated zucchini and mix well.

Spoon the cake batter into the pan and bake in the preheated oven for 35–45 minutes. Test the centre of the cake with a skewer—when it comes out clean the cake is ready. Remove the cake from the pan and leave to cool, then cut into squares.

zucchini, lemon thyme, & feta loaf

2½ cups all-purpose flour

2 tablespoons baking powder

1 teaspoon salt

¾ cup whole milk

⅔ cup extra virgin olive oil

2 eggs, beaten

1 large zucchini, coarsely grated

4 oz. feta, crumbled

2 fresh lemon thyme sprigs, leaves only

freshly ground black pepper

a 9 x 5 x 3-inch loaf pan, lined with baking parchment

makes 1 large loaf

Preheat the oven to 350°F.

Sift the flour, baking powder, and salt into a large bowl and season with freshly ground black pepper.

In a large measuring cup, combine the milk and oil and beat in the eggs. Stir into the dry ingredients along with the zucchini, two-thirds of the feta, and half the thyme leaves. Stir until there are no more floury pockets but don't overbeat or you'll make the mixture tough. Spoon into the prepared loaf pan. Scatter over the remaining feta and thyme. Bake in the preheated oven for 1–1¼ hours, or until a skewer inserted in the centre comes out clean.

Remove from the oven and let cool for 10 minutes in the pan, then turn out onto a wire rack to cool completely.

mushrooms

roasted mushrooms with spiced squash stuffing

mushroom soup with madeira & hazelnuts

mushroom & thyme ragu with

hand-torn pasta 🌿 mushroom tart

baked mushrooms with manchego béchamel

sautéed mushrooms & lentils with bacon

garlic mushrooms & goat cheese on toast

These two dishes are full of warm, comforting flavors. Serve the roasted mushrooms with rice pilaf and maybe a spinach salad. Use a squash with a dryish, chestnutty flesh such as Kabocha or Crown Prince. Mushrooms and their earthiness blend really well with the sweet tang of Madeira wine, with the hazelnuts adding a lovely thickness to the soup.

roasted mushrooms with spiced squash stuffing

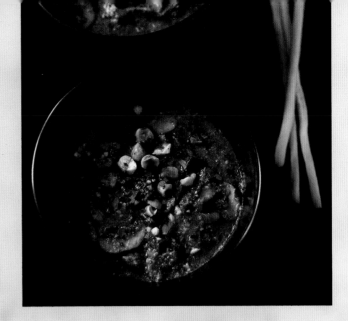

1 small squash (about 2 lbs.), peeled, seeded, and cubed

5–6 tablespoons olive oil

a small bunch of fresh thyme

¼ teaspoon dried hot pepper flakes

1 garlic clove, chopped

14-oz. can chickpeas, drained

½–1 teaspoon ground toasted cumin seeds

freshly squeezed lemon juice, to taste

1–2 tablespoons chopped flatleaf parsley

1–2 tablespoons crème fraîche or heavy cream (optional)

8 large, flat portobello mushrooms, stalks removed

4 tablespoons toasted pumpkin seeds

sea salt and freshly ground black pepper

for the sauce

1 garlic clove

a pinch of coarse sea salt

3–4 tablespoons tahini

freshly squeezed lemon juice, to taste

4–5 tablespoons natural yogurt

1 tablespoon freshly chopped mint

serves 4

Preheat the oven to 425°F. Toss the squash with 3 tablespoons of the oil, 1 teaspoon chopped thyme, the hot pepper flakes, and garlic. Season and put on a baking sheet. Cover with foil and cook in the preheated oven for about 30 minutes until tender, then uncover and cook for a further 10 minutes. Let cool and put in a food processor with the chickpeas. Whizz to make a rough purée. Season to taste with salt, pepper, cumin, and lemon juice, then stir in the parsley. If the purée is very dry, add the crème fraîche or a little water.

Meanwhile, put the mushrooms, gill-side uppermost, on an oiled baking sheet. Season and sprinkle with a few thyme leaves. Drizzle with the remaining oil and a good squeeze of lemon juice. Roast, uncovered, in the preheated oven for 15 minutes until just cooked. Remove from the oven and reduce the heat to 375°F.

Distribute the stuffing evenly between the mushrooms. Scatter with the pumpkin seeds and a few thyme sprigs. Spoon over a little of the mushroom cooking juices, then return them to the oven for 10 minutes to heat through. To make the sauce, mash the garlic with the salt in a bowl, then gradually work in 3 tablespoons tahini, followed by 1 tablespoon lemon juice. When smooth, gradually work in the yogurt, then taste and add more lemon juice and/or tahini as necessary. Stir in the mint and serve with the mushrooms.

mushroom soup with madeira & hazelnuts

3 tablespoons butter

1 large onion, chopped

3 garlic cloves, crushed

3 tablespoons blanched hazelnuts

3 tablespoons freshly chopped parsley

12 oz. brown mushrooms, sliced

1 oz. dried porcini mushrooms

4 cups hot vegetable or chicken stock

6 tablespoons Madeira

serves 4–6

Melt the butter in a large saucepan and add the onion and garlic. Cover and cook over low heat for 10 minutes, or until soft. Stir occasionally so that they don't color. Meanwhile, toast the hazelnuts in a dry skillet and roughly chop, then set aside.

Add half the parsley and all the mushrooms to the saucepan and turn the heat up to medium. Cover and cook, stirring, for 15 minutes until they are softened.

Put the dried mushrooms in a heatproof bowl with ½ cup of the hot stock and set aside to soak for about 15 minutes to rehydrate.

Add the Madeira to the pan and cook until it evaporates. Add the remaining stock and the dried mushrooms with their soaking liquid, cover, and cook for 10 minutes.

Transfer half the soup to a blender, along with half the hazelnuts and liquidize until smooth, then stir back into the pan and heat through. Divide the soup between 4–6 bowls and scatter the remaining parsley and toasted hazelnuts over the top.

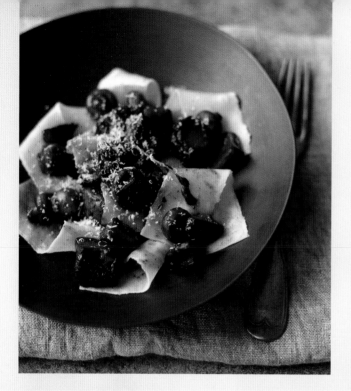

Many exotic mushroom varieties are available year-round. These recipes use a mixture, giving the dishes a roundness of flavor. In the pasta, the meaty field mushrooms go hand in hand with the other comforting, rich flavors like fresh thyme, red wine, and cinnamon. If you like to pick your own mushrooms, feel free to experiment with your selection, but you can just as easily use any seasonal variety you might find at your local farmers' market.

mushroom tart

1 Pizza Dough recipe
(see page 56)

½ oz. dried porcini mushrooms

1 large red onion, cubed

2 tablespoons olive oil,
plus extra to drizzle

2 tablespoons water

1 teaspoon salt

½ teaspoon crushed black
pepper

1 teaspoon freshly chopped
thyme, plus extra whole sprigs
to decorate

2 garlic cloves, chopped

5 oz. button mushrooms
(halved if big)

7 oz. cremini mushrooms,
sliced about ¼ inch thick

¾ cup light cream

1 large egg, beaten

a 8 x 10-inch fluted tart pan,
greased

serves 6

Put the porcini mushrooms in a bowl of warm water and let soak for 20 minutes. Drain, chop, and set aside.

Preheat the oven to 400ºF.

Put the onion, oil, and water in a skillet and sauté over low heat for about 10 minutes, or until soft and the water has evaporated. Remove from the heat and stir in the salt, pepper, thyme, garlic, and porcini mushrooms. Mix well and set aside.

Put the fresh mushrooms in a roasting pan, drizzle with oil, and cover the pan with aluminum foil. Roast in the preheated oven for 10 minutes. Remove from the oven and leave to cool for 10 minutes. Drain any excess juice from the mushrooms, then stir them into the onion mixture.

Reduce the oven temperature to 325ºF.

Line the tart pan with the Pizza Dough but do not trim the edges yet.

Mix together the cream and egg in a bowl, then pour half into the tart crust. Spread the mixed vegetables over the tart, then pour in the remaining cream mixture. Now trim the excess dough neatly around the edges.

Bake in the preheated oven for 25–30 minutes. Remove from the oven and leave to cool, then decorate with a few sprigs of thyme. Serve warm or cold.

mushroom & thyme ragu with hand-torn pasta

2 tablespoons light olive oil

2 tablespoons butter

1 onion, chopped

2 garlic cloves, chopped

3 large field mushrooms, caps
removed and cut into 1-inch
pieces

6 oz. button mushrooms

3 oz. fresh shiitake
mushrooms, quartered

3 fresh thyme sprigs

1 cup red wine

1 cinnamon stick

1 cup vegetable or beef stock

14 oz. fresh lasagne sheets,
cut or torn into thick strips

sea salt and freshly ground
black pepper

freshly grated Parmesan
cheese, to serve

serves 4

Heat the oil and butter in a heavy-based saucepan over medium heat. Add the onion and garlic and cook for 4–5 minutes, until the onions have softened. Increase the heat to high, add the mushrooms and thyme, and cook for a further 8–10 minutes, stirring often, until the mushrooms darken and soften.

Add the red wine and cinnamon to the pan and boil for 5 minutes. Pour in the stock and season well with sea salt and black pepper. Reduce the heat and gently simmer the mixture for 35–40 minutes.

Cook the pasta in a saucepan of boiling water for 2–3 minutes, until it rises to the surface. Drain well and place in serving bowls. Spoon the mushroom sauce on top and sprinkle with Parmesan to serve.

Tapas is casual, shared food at its very best and mushrooms are very well suited to the small plates style of cooking. They really are nature's cups just waiting to be filled. Look for mushrooms that will be two to three small mouthfuls when cooked— wild cremini mushrooms or the large portobello mushrooms are both ideal. These are very rich, so a crisp fennel salad is the perfect accompaniment.

baked mushrooms with manchego béchamel

Put the butter in a small saucepan and cook over high heat until it is melted and sizzling. Before the butter burns, add the flour and stir quickly to form a thick paste. Remove from the heat and add a little of the milk, stirring constantly until thick and smooth. Return the pan to medium heat and add the remaining milk, whisking constantly until all the milk is incorporated and the mixture is smooth and thick. Remove from the heat and leave cool.

Preheat the oven to 425°F. Remove the stalks from the mushrooms and sit the mushrooms in a small baking dish, gill-side up. Spoon the cheese sauce into the caps and sprinkle the paprika over the top. Cook in the preheated oven for 20 minutes, until the mushrooms are soft and the sauce is golden and bubbling.

While the mushrooms are cooking, slice the fennel bulb as finely as possible, chop the fronds and put in a bowl with the parsley, oil, and lemon juice. Toss to combine, season to taste, and serve with the warm mushrooms.

2 teaspoons butter

2 teaspoons plain flour

½ cup whole milk

½ cup finely grated Manchego cheese

12 wide, flat mushrooms

¼ teaspoon smoked paprika (pimentón)

fennel salad

1 small fennel bulb

a handful of fresh flatleaf parsley leaves

2 teaspoons olive oil

2 teaspoons freshly squeezed lemon juice

sea salt and freshly ground black pepper

serves 4–6

* tip

Although mushroom types are detailed for guidance, the different mushroom varieties can often be used interchangeably, so you can work around what you have available. If you need to slice a lot of mushrooms, try using an egg slicer to make quick work of the job.

The rich, earthy taste of mushrooms makes them perfect for these two rustic dishes. Mushrooms and lentils go fabulously with pork in this hearty hotpot. Small brown lentils stay firm during cooking, but the big green ones called castellanas have a good flavor too. For a quick brunch, garlicky mushrooms are great partnered with soft, creamy goat cheese. The kind of cheese you are looking for is a soft fresh cheese, not aged, so it will not have a rind. You could also use ricotta if you like. Seek out a good, sturdy rustic bread such as sourdough for this dish to prevent the underneath going soggy.

sautéed mushrooms & lentils with bacon

1¼ cups small lentils, rinsed

3 tablespoons extra virgin olive oil

1 onion, finely chopped

1 garlic clove, crushed

2 tablespoons butter

4 oz. small cremini mushrooms

4 oz. oyster mushrooms, cut in half if large

3 tablespoons freshly chopped flatleaf parsley

1 teaspoon freshly squeezed lemon juice

fine sea salt and freshly ground black pepper

6–12 slices streaky bacon

leaves from a small bunch of fresh flatleaf parsley, half chopped, the rest left whole, to serve

serves 6

Put the lentils in a saucepan, cover with 1 quart cold water and bring to a boil. Lower the heat and simmer for about 35 minutes or until tender (the time will depend on the age of the lentils). Drain.

Heat 2 tablespoons of the oil in a skillet, add the onion and garlic, and fry for about 10 minutes until soft and pale golden. Add the butter, the remaining oil, and the mushrooms. Stir-fry until the mushrooms are just cooked. Add the lentils, chopped parsley, lemon juice, salt, and pepper and continue to stir until heated all the way through.

Meanwhile, broil the bacon until crisp. Serve the lentils topped with the parsley and 1–2 slices of bacon per serving.

garlic mushrooms & goat cheese on toast

8 brown mushrooms

3 garlic cloves, crushed

3 tablespoons olive oil

3 tablespoons pine nuts

2 tablespoons balsamic vinegar

4 slices of sourdough bread

5 oz. fresh goat cheese

fresh tarragon, to serve

sea salt and freshly ground black pepper

serves 4

Preheat the oven to 400°F.

Put the mushrooms, garlic, and oil in a roasting pan. Toss well and season. Roast in the preheated oven for 15 minutes, until tender. Stir in the pine nuts and balsamic vinegar halfway through roasting.

Just before the mushrooms are ready, toast the slices of sourdough bread and spread with the goat cheese. Place the mushrooms on top, stalk side up, scatter with the tarragon, and serve immediately. Add more seasoning, if necessary.

tree fruits

praline apple strudel ❦ apple & blueberry tarts

apple & carrot bread with walnuts

apple, pear, & ginger chutney ❦ apple, red onion, & dried

cherry chutney ❦ apple butter ❦ apple lemonade

toffee apples ❦ roast apples & parsnips

poached pear tiramisù ❦ individual pear, maple, &

pecan cobblers ❦ frosted pear, zucchini, & carrot cake

pickled pears with tamarind & ginger

roasted pear relish ❦ warm pear, gorgonzola, & pecan

tartlets with maple drizzle ❦ pan plum crumble

plum fudge puddings ❦ greengage jam

plum & apple tart ❦ free-form caramelized peach tart

roasted mascarpone peaches ❦ peach halves in brandy with

star anise ❦ upside-down peach cake ❦ nectarine, blueberry,

& lavender tray bake ❦ nectarine & pistachio

summer crumble ❦ buttered apricot betty

apricot & almond slump ❦ white chocolate & apricot roulade

cherry, peach, & vanilla shortcake ❦ cherry & ricotta strudel

cherry & almond clafoutis ❦ italian fig conserve

spiced muscat figs

The end of the summer needn't mean the end of gloriously fresh, vibrant desserts. The chances are that your apple trees will be laden with fruit, so here are apples two ways—in individual tarts, using sweet eating apples and juicy blueberries, combined with vanilla; and in a rustic strudel, which is lifted well above the ordinary with the addition of it's secret ingredient—praline powder.

praline apple strudel

1 lb. tart eating apples, such as Cox's or Braeburn, peeled, cored, and chopped

¼ cup dried fruit, such as golden raisins, cranberries or sour cherries

½ cup light brown sugar

1 teaspoon ground cinnamon

1 tablespoon unsalted butter

6 sheets phyllo pastry (thawed if frozen)

4 tablespoons unsalted butter, melted

confectioners' sugar, to dust

whipped cream or crème fraîche, to serve

for the praline

½ cup shelled pecans

½ cup sugar

a baking sheet, lined with baking parchment

serves 6–8

To make the praline, combine the pecans and sugar in a non-stick heavy-based skillet and cook over medium/high heat, stirring constantly, until the sugar hardens and coats the nuts. Transfer to a plate to cool, then process in a coffee grinder or small food processor until ground to a coarse powder. Set aside.

In a large saucepan, combine the apples, dried fruit, brown sugar, cinnamon, and 1 tablespoon butter. Cook over medium heat until the apples are soft and the juices have evaporated, about 15 minutes. Remove from the heat and let cool.

Preheat the oven to 375°F.

Put 2 sheets of phyllo on the prepared baking sheet and brush with some melted butter. Sprinkle with a little praline. Top with 2 more sheets of phyllo and a little more praline. Top with 2 more sheets of phyllo. Spread the apple mixture in an even layer over the top sheet of phyllo. Sprinkle with more praline mixture, then carefully roll up from a long end, like a Swiss roll. Use the paper to help you roll, if necessary. The seam side needs to be on the bottom. Brush with a little more melted butter, sprinkle with any remaining praline, and bake in the preheated oven until crisp and golden, about 25–35 minutes.

Remove from the oven and let cool slightly. Dust with a little confectioners' sugar, slice, and serve warm with whipped cream or crème fraîche.

apple & blueberry tarts

12 oz. sheet ready-rolled puff pastry, defrosted if frozen, cut into 4 squares each about 5 inches square

2 tablespoons sugar

1 vanilla bean, cut in half lengthwise

3 sweet dessert apples, cored and cut into 10–12 thin wedges

1 basket blueberries

cream, to serve

a baking sheet, lined with baking parchment

serves 4

Preheat the oven to 425°F.

Place the puff pastry squares on a the prepared baking sheet.

Put the sugar and 2 tablespoons water in a saucepan and bring to a boil, stirring until the sugar dissolves. Scrape the seeds from the vanilla bean directly into the sugar syrup, stirring to combine.

Add the apple slices to the pan, reduce the heat to medium, and cook for 4–5 minutes, turning the apples so they cook evenly. Add the blueberries and gently stir to coat in the sweet syrup. Arrange the apples and blueberries on top of each pastry square. Bake in the preheated oven for 18–20 minutes, until the pastry is puffed and golden.

Serve warm with the cream spooned over the top.

This delicious, rustic bread is very simple to make. One large loaf goes a long way and keeps well, so it is ideal if you just want something freshly baked around the house for a few days. It is very nice plain, or spread with butter or cream cheese if you are feeling indulgent.

apple & carrot bread with walnuts

Preheat the oven to 350°F.

In a mixing bowl, combine the flour, sugar, baking powder, salt, cinnamon, nutmeg, ginger, and allspice. Set aside.

In a separate bowl, mix together the apple juice, melted butter, and eggs. Gently fold this mixture into the flour mixture to combine. Use your hands to squeeze every last drop of moisture from the grated apple and carrots then add to the mixture, along with the walnuts and stir just to combine.

Transfer the mixture to the prepared loaf pan and level the top. Bake in the preheated oven until a skewer inserted in the centre of the cake comes out clean, about 1–1¼ hours.

Leave the cake to cool in the pan for a few minutes then turn out onto a wire rack to cool. Slice as you would bread to serve. The cake will keep in an airtight container for 4–5 days.

1¾ cups all-purpose flour

¾ cup light brown sugar

1 tablespoon baking powder

a pinch of fine sea salt

1 teaspoon ground cinnamon

½ teaspoon ground nutmeg

¼ teaspoon each ground ginger and allspice

⅔ cup apple juice

5 tablespoons unsalted butter, melted

2 large eggs, beaten

1 large tart cooking apple, such as Bramley, peeled, cored and grated

1 cup grated carrot

½ cup walnuts, coarsely chopped

a 9 x 5 x 4-inch loaf pan (2 lbs. capacity), buttered

serves 6–8

Homemade chutneys are very useful to keep on hand. A great way to use fresh produce, they are ideal served with cheese and biscuits or as part of a ploughman's lunch, and they are perfect with roast meats—both hot and cold. They also make a tasty sandwich ingredient. The apple, pear, and ginger chutney is especially suited to pork, while the apple, red onion, and dried cherry chutney goes very well with chicken, turkey, and even duck.

apple, pear, & ginger chutney

3 eating apples, such as Golden Delicious, peeled, cored, and cubed

2 large ripe pears, peeled, cored, and cubed

1 large white onion, finely chopped

1½ cups cider vinegar

1½ cups light brown sugar

¾ cup golden raisins or raisins

5-oz. piece of fresh ginger, peeled and finely chopped

½ teaspoon sea salt

½ teaspoon dried hot pepper flakes

makes 4–5 cups

In a large non-reactive saucepan, combine the apples, pears, onion, vinegar, sugar, golden raisins, ginger, salt, and hot pepper flakes. Cook over medium heat, stirring occasionally, until thick, about 30–40 minutes.

Transfer the chutney to a spotlessly clean and dry, sealable airtight container. It will keep in the fridge for up to 2 weeks.

apple, red onion, & dried cherry chutney

3 eating apples, such as Golden Delicious, peeled, cored, and cubed

1 large or 2 medium red onions, halved and sliced

1 heaping cup dried sour cherries

2 cups cider vinegar

3 tablespoons light brown sugar

¼ teaspoon ground cloves

¼ teaspoon sea salt

freshly ground black pepper

makes 2–3 cups

In a large non-reactive saucepan, combine the apples, onion, dried cherries, vinegar, sugar, cloves, salt, and a few grinds of black pepper. Cook over medium heat, stirring occasionally, until thick, about 30–40 minutes.

Transfer the chutney to a spotlessly clean and dry, sealable airtight container. It will keep in the fridge for up to 2 weeks.

apple butter

3 lbs. mixed apples, such as Braeburn, Cox's or Bramley, peeled, cored, and chopped

¾ cup runny honey

1 cup sugar

2 tablespoons freshly squeezed lemon juice

1 teaspoon ground cinnamon

½ teaspoon ground cloves

1 cup apple juice

makes about 3½ lbs.

Combine all the ingredients in a large non-reactive saucepan. Bring to a boil, stirring occasionally. Lower the heat and simmer, stirring occasionally, and using a wooden spoon, crush the apples, until thick, about 20–25 minutes. Remove from the heat.

Transfer the jam to a spotlessly clean and dry, sealable airtight container. It will keep in the fridge for 7–10 days. Alternatively, spoon into hot, dry sterilized jars while hot (see note on page 4). Leave to cool, then seal. The jam will keep for 3–4 weeks if correctly sealed. Use as you would any fruit preserve.

apple lemonade

2–3 cooking apples, unpeeled, chopped into small pieces

sugar, to taste

freshly squeezed juice of 1 lemon

ice, to serve

sparkling mineral water, to serve

serves 4

Put the apples into a saucepan, cover with cold water, bring to a boil and simmer until soft. Strain, pressing the pulp through the strainer with a spoon. Add sugar to taste, stir until dissolved, then leave to cool.

To serve, fill a pitcher with ice, half-fill the glass with the apple juice, add the lemon juice, and top with mineral water.

toffee apples

8 small apples, such as Cox's

1½ cups sugar

2 tablespoons golden syrup

freshly squeezed juice of ½ lemon

finely chopped mixed nuts and edible sprinkles, for dipping (optional)

8 wooden skewers or lolly sticks

a large sheet of baking parchment

makes 8

Wash and thoroughly dry each apple. Carefully push a wooden skewer or popsicle stick into the stalk end of each apple.

Put the sugar, golden syrup, and ½ cup water in a heavy-based saucepan set over low heat. Leave until the sugar has completely dissolved then turn up the heat and simmer until the toffee turns an amber color.

Remove the pan from the heat. Add the lemon juice—taking care as the hot toffee may splutter. Working quickly, dip each apple into the toffee and swirl it around until evenly coated.

Leave to cool for 30 seconds, then dip the bottoms of the apples in mixed nuts or sprinkles, if using. Sit the apples on the baking parchment to harden. Serve on the same day.

roast apples & parsnips

2 tablespoons olive oil

½ teaspoon dried sage

½ teaspoon salt

1 eating apple, cut into wedges

2 parsnips, about 12 oz., peeled and cut into wedges

1 tablespoon freshly chopped flatleaf parsley

serves 4

Preheat the oven to 425°F.

Put the oil, sage, and salt in a plastic bag, then add the apple and parsnips. Roll them around until well coated with oil. Empty the bag onto a baking sheet and roast in the preheated oven for 30 minutes, turning the vegetables every 10 minutes. Sprinkle with parsley, mix well, and serve.

Tiramisù (which literally translates from the Italian as pick-me-up) must be one of the best-loved desserts in the world. It has all the essential elements of a perfect pudding—alcohol, creamy custard, and cocoa. Pears work particularly well with anything sweet, creamy and cheesey so mascarpone makes an ideal partner. Do choose your pears carefully. Soft and sweet varieties do not poach well and will end up as an overly sweet mush. Bosc are good, but any firm brown variety will work.

poached pear tiramisù

6–8 savoiardi (ladyfinger cookies)

1 cup Marsala or brandy

½ cup sugar

2 firm brown pears (such as Bosc), peeled, cored, and cut into eighths

2 egg whites

4 egg yolks

1 cup mascarpone cheese

cocoa powder, for dusting

4 individual serving dishes

serves 6

Line the bottom of each serving dish with savoiardi, breaking them in order to fit them in.

Put the Marsala or brandy, half of the sugar, and ½ cup water in a non-stick skillet and cook over high heat until the mixture boils, stirring until the sugar has dissolved. Add the pears and cook on a gentle simmer for 20 minutes, turning them often, until they are soft and glossy and there is about half of the liquid remaining.

Lay the pears on top of the savoiardi and pour over the poaching liquid. Using electric beaters, beat the egg whites until firm peaks form. Beat the egg yolks with the remaining sugar for 4–5 minutes, until they are pale in color and doubled in size, then beat the mascarpone into the yolks until smooth.

Using a large spoon, fold the egg whites into the yolk and sugar mixture and spoon this over the pears. Cover each dish with plastic wrap and refrigerate until ready to serve.

Dust each one with a little cocoa powder just before serving.

individual pear, maple, & pecan cobblers

4 small ripe pears

finely grated zest and freshly squeezed juice of ½ a lemon

4 tablespoons maple syrup

cobbler topping

½ stick unsalted butter, chilled

1¾ cups self-rising flour

a pinch of salt

3 tablespoons maple syrup

1 scant cup whole milk

½ cup roughly chopped pecan nuts

heavy cream or Greek yogurt, to serve

4 individual ovenproof ramekins or similar

a fluted 2-inch cookie cutter

serves 4

These cheeky little pear desserts will raise a smile as you bring them to the table. Use deep ramekins to achieve the impressive starry effect. They look spectacular—and they taste just as good as they look.

Preheat the oven to 425°F.

Peel and core the pears, then slice them thickly lengthwise (or quarter if small and thin). Put the pears into a saucepan with the lemon zest and juice and the maple syrup. Poach gently for 10 minutes until the fruit is almost tender. Set aside.

To make the topping, rub the butter into the flour and salt until it resembles fine breadcrumbs. Stir the maple syrup into the milk and add ⅔ cup only to the flour, mixing with a blunt knife to form a fairly soft, sticky dough. Tip out onto a flour-dusted work surface and roll out until 1 inch thick. Cut out rounds using the cookie cutter.

Take 4 ramekins and arrange the pear slices around the edge like a star, with the thicker ends in the centre of the dish and the thinner ends pointing upwards out of the dishes. Spoon the juice evenly over the pears and anchor them with a round of cobbler dough placed lightly in the centre. Brush the top of the cobblers with the remaining milk and sprinkle with the chopped nuts. Place the ramekins on a baking sheet and bake in the preheated oven for 10–15 minutes, until the cobbler dough is puffed golden brown, and the pears just browning at their tips. Serve hot with heavy cream or Greek yogurt.

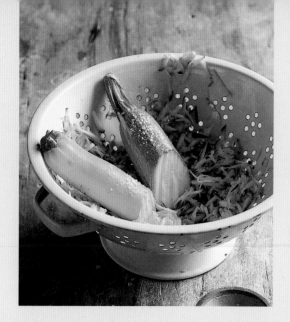

frosted pear, zucchini, & carrot cake

This is a true celebration of your garden produce, and by packing pears, zucchini, and carrots into this cake, you can be sure it will be deliciously moist. Coconut oil often solidifies in its container, so immerse the pot or jar in a bowl of hot water, from the kettle, for about 10 minutes to melt the oil. If you want to make this cake completely dairy-free, replace the butter, cream cheese, and yogurt in the frosting with 6½ oz. soya cream cheese, sweetened with 2 tablespoons confectioners' sugar. This cake will store well for a few days, but even longer if kept in an airtight container in the fridge. Serve it at room temperature.

1½ cups all-purpose flour

¾ cup spelt flour

1 slightly rounded teaspoon baking powder

1 teaspoon baking soda

1 tablespoon ground cinnamon

2 pinches of ground cloves

4 large eggs

1⅓ cup light muscovado or packed light brown sugar

1 cup virgin coconut oil or canola oil

2 medium pears, cored and chopped (no need to peel)

1 cup grated carrots (no need to peel)

⅔ cup grated zucchini (no need to peel)

⅔ cup golden raisins

1 cup walnut or pecan pieces

poppy seed frosting

5 tablespoons unsalted butter, very soft

6½ oz. cream cheese, chilled

⅓ cup Greek yogurt, chilled

1¼ cups confectioners' sugar, sifted

1 tablespoon poppy seeds

two 8-inch round cake pans, lightly buttered and base-lined with baking parchment

serves 12

Preheat the oven to 350°F.

Sift the flours, baking powder, and baking soda into the bowl of an electric mixer (or use a large mixing bowl and an electric whisk). Tip any spelt left in the sieve into the bowl too. Add the cinnamon, cloves, eggs, sugar, and oil. Mix together.

In another bowl, mix the pears, carrots, zucchini, golden raisins, and nuts. Using a large metal spoon, fold these ingredients into the cake batter, making sure everything is thoroughly combined.

Divide the mixture between the prepared pans and spread it evenly with a spatula. Bake in the preheated oven for 40–45 minutes, or until risen, golden, and set in the centre. Let cool in the pans.

To make the poppy seed frosting, whisk together the butter and cream cheese, add the yogurt and confectioners' sugar, and whisk again—an electric whisk makes quick work of this. Stir in the poppy seeds, then refrigerate until needed.

Tip the cold cakes out of the pans and peel off the parchment paper. Place one cake on a board or serving plate, bottom-side uppermost. Spread half the frosting over it. Put the other cake on top, top-side uppermost, and spread the remaining frosting over the top.

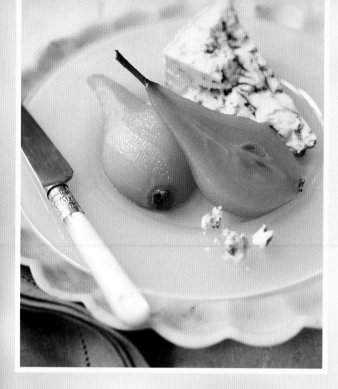

It's not just apples that go well with pork—if you have plenty of pears, try making this relish to serve with a roast (it also works well with poultry). And if there's fruit left over, preserve it for the winter months. Pickled fruits, such as these delicious pears with tamarind and ginger, can be made with all kinds of vinegars; red and white wine, cider, perry, or rice. This recipe uses dark malt vinegar because some varieties of pear turn brown when preserved. The flavor is not impaired, nor the texture of the fruit, but the color is a little off-putting. If you use dark malt vinegar, the change of color goes unnoticed. The combination of spices used in this recipe comes originally from the Middle East, but try others such as chile, dill, allspice, or coriander seeds. If you are unable to get hold of tamarind paste, simply omit it.

pickled pears with tamarind & ginger

2 cups malt or cider vinegar (see above)

2 tablespoons finely grated fresh ginger

3 garlic cloves, crushed

3 heaping teaspoons tamarind paste

1½ teaspoons cumin seeds

a pinch of salt

1 cup soft brown sugar

2 lbs. firm pears

3 sealable, sterilized, ½ quart jars or a 1½ quart jar (see note on page 4)

makes 1½ quarts

Put the vinegar, ginger, garlic, tamarind paste, cumin seeds, salt, and sugar in a pan and bring slowly to simmering point. Cook over low heat until the sugar has dissolved, then boil for 5 minutes.

Meanwhile, peel the pears, cut in half, and pack into the warmed jars. Fill to the brim with the reduced vinegar. If there isn't enough vinegar to cover the fruit, simply boil up extra vinegar, adding 3 tablespoons sugar to every ½ cup vinegar, and top up the jars. Seal the jars and label when cold.

Keep at least 3 months before opening. Serve with cheese at the end of a meal, or as part of a cured meat starter, with cold cooked meats, ham, game, or pies.

*Variation You could also preserve peaches, figs, or quinces in this way. Peaches and figs do not need peeling prior to pickling—pears and quinces do.

roasted pear relish

4 ripe pears, peeled, halved, and cored

2 tablespoons freshly squeezed lemon juice

1 tablespoon light brown sugar

¼ cup sugar

¾ teaspoon ground cinnamon

¼ teaspoon ground cloves

¼ cup pure maple syrup

1 small red onion, cut into ½-inch slices

1 tablespoon peeled and grated fresh ginger

5 tablespoons raisins

½ cup cider vinegar

1 teaspoon dried hot pepper flakes (optional)

vegetable oil, for brushing

serves 4–6

Preheat the oven to 350°F.

Brush a baking sheet with vegetable oil. In a bowl, combine the pears, lemon juice, both the sugars, cinnamon, and cloves and mix well to coat the pears. Arrange the pears cut-side down on the sheet and brush with a little more oil. Roast in the preheated oven until caramelized, about 45 minutes. When the pears are cool enough to handle, cut into small cubes.

Meanwhile, put the remaining ingredients in a non-reactive saucepan and bring to a boil. Reduce the heat and simmer, uncovered, for 5 minutes. Remove from the heat and let cool. Add the cubed pears to the onion mixture and mix well. Cover and refrigerate for at least 1 day before serving. Transfer the relish to a spotlessly clean and dry, sealable airtight container. It will keep in the fridge for up to 10 days.

warm pear, gorgonzola, & pecan tartlets with maple drizzle

12-oz. sheet ready-rolled
puff pastry dough

1 egg, lightly beaten

7 oz. Gorgonzola cheese

4 tablespoons heavy cream

cayenne pepper

½ cup shelled pecan nuts
or walnuts

2–3 ripe pears

6 teaspoons maple syrup

serves 6

Preheat the oven to 425°F.

Take the pastry out of the fridge and leave to warm up a little for
10–15 minutes.

Unroll the pastry, cut it in half horizontally, then cut each of the
halves into 3 to make 6 equal-sized pieces. With the tip of a sharp
knife, score round each of the squares about ⅔ inch from the edge
to make a border. Lightly brush the border with beaten egg, taking
care not to brush over the cut you've made (otherwise the pastry
won't puff up around the edge of the tartlets).

Put the Gorgonzola in a bowl and break up roughly with a fork, then
stir in the cream. Season with a little cayenne pepper and spread
over the bases of the tartlets, taking care not to cover the border.
Roughly break up the pecan nuts and divide between the tartlets.
Peel, core, and quarter the pears, cut each quarter into 3 wedges
and lay them in overlapping slices on top of the cheese and nuts.
Drizzle a teaspoonful of maple syrup over each tart and bake in the
preheated oven for 15–20 minutes until the pastry is well browned
and puffed up. Leave to cool for 5 minutes before serving.

Pears have a natural affinity with blue cheese and
are a classic combination, especially with nuts added
too. These mouthwatering golden tartlets are a
cheese course and dessert rolled into one—a fabulous
finale for a dinner party.

pears 149

Here are sweet, sticky plum fudge puddings and a comforting crumble that is cooked under the broiler. Plum crumble is a classic, but you could use any fruit you have—just be aware that soft summer berries will need very little time in the skillet, while apples and pears will require a little longer.

pan plum crumble

¾ cup freshly squeezed orange juice

2 tablespoons superfine sugar

6 ripe plums, halved and pitted

¾ cup self-rising flour

⅓ cup soft brown sugar

½ cup rolled oats

4 tablespoons unsalted butter, cubed and chilled

vanilla ice cream, to serve

serves 4–6

Put the orange juice and superfine sugar in a small skillet and set it over high heat. Bring the mixture to a boil, then reduce the heat to medium. Add the plums, cut-side down, and cook for 5 minutes. Turn the plums over and cook for a further 5 minutes, until they have softened yet still retain their shape and the liquid has almost evaporated. Remove the skillet from the heat and set aside.

Preheat the broiler to medium.

Put the flour, brown sugar, and oats in a bowl and mix just to combine. Add the butter and use your fingertips to rub it into the dry ingredients.

Sprinkle the mixture evenly over the plums and slide the skillet under the hot broiler for 2–3 minutes, until the crumble is golden. Serve warm with a scoop of vanilla ice cream.

plum fudge puddings

4 tablespoons unsalted butter

4–5 tablespoons honey

2 tablespoons heavy cream

2 tablespoons brown sugar

1 teaspoon apple pie spice or a pinch of cinnamon plus a little freshly grated nutmeg

1½ cups fresh white breadcrumbs

2 ripe plums, halved, pitted, and thinly sliced

crème fraîche, to serve

4 ramekins, ⅔ cup each

serves 4

Preheat the oven to 400°F.

Put the butter, honey, and cream into a saucepan and heat until melted. Put the sugar, spice, and breadcrumbs into a bowl and mix thoroughly.

Divide half the buttery fudge mixture between the ramekin dishes and top with a layer of plum slices and half the breadcrumb mix. Add the remaining plums and breadcrumbs, then spoon over the remaining sauce.

Set the ramekins on a baking sheet and bake in the preheated oven for 20 minutes. Remove from the oven and let cool for 5 minutes, then carefully unmould the puddings and serve with a spoonful of crème fraîche.

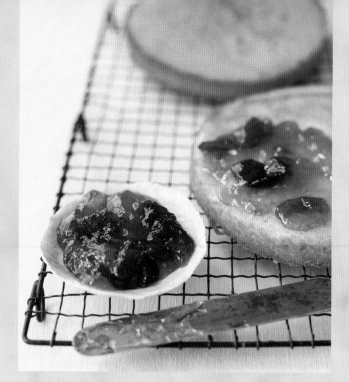

greengage jam

3 lbs. greengages or other plums

1 large whole star anise

7½ cups sugar

2 clean, sealable, sterilized jars, ½ quart each

makes 1 pint–1 quart

Rinse the fruit, remove the stalks, and let dry naturally in the sun. Put the fruit in a large saucepan with the star anise and ½ cup water and simmer gently to soften the skins, taking care not to let the fruit become mushy.

Discard the star anise. Add the sugar and continue to simmer over low heat to dissolve the sugar, stirring all the time. Bring to a boil and remove as many stones as come to the surface. Boil rapidly until setting point is reached (see page 166), 5–10 minutes.

If the jam is not ready, put the pan back on the heat to boil for a few minutes longer and test again. Repeat this process if necessary and remember to take the jam off the heat while testing, because over-boiling will ruin it.

When setting point has been reached, skim the jam with a perforated skimmer, stir it well and let stand for 20 minutes for the fruit to settle. Stir and ladle into jars. Seal at once with waxed paper discs and close with a lid or appropriate cover.

Let cool, label, and store in a cool, dark cupboard until required.

Variation Santa Rosa Jam

If using large plum varieties such as Santa Rosa, it may be a good idea to cut the plums in half and remove the pits before cooking.

Greengage jam is an English country classic, and the perfect way to savor a bumper crop. Plum and aniseed makes a wonderful combination, whether for jam, chutney, bottling, stewing, pies, crumbles, or fools. Cinnamon and cloves also work well if aniseed is not a favorite of yours, but do try it first. Greengages make a dark golden-yellow jam, but you can use other plum varieties to make jams that vary in color from yellow to pink or purple. If you grow a sweet plum variety, they can also be used to bake this irresistible plum tart, perfectly combined with sharp, strongly flavored apples. This one has plenty of fruit filling, which makes it wonderfully juicy.

plum & apple tart

3 tablespoons unsalted butter, at room temperature

a scant ½ cup sugar

1 egg

1½ teaspoons baking powder

¾ cup all-purpose flour

12 oz. ready-rolled sweet shortcrust pastry, defrosted if frozen

10 Santa Rosa plums, pitted and halved

2 Bramley apples, cored and sliced

3 tablespoons apricot jam, to glaze (optional)

a 9-inch loose-based fluted tart pan, greased

makes about 8 slices

Preheat the oven to 325°F.

To make the cake batter, put the butter and sugar in a mixing bowl and mix with an electric whisk to combine. Mix in the egg and baking powder with the whisk, then gently fold in the flour by hand until evenly combined.

Line the tart pan with the shortcrust pastry dough and trim the excess dough neatly around the edges. Spoon the cake batter into the tart crust and spread evenly. Scatter the plums and apples all over the mixture.

Bake in the preheated oven for 40 minutes. When the tart is ready, the fruit will have sunk a little and the cake will have risen up in parts and be golden. Remove from the oven and leave to cool for a few minutes.

In the meantime, put the apricot jam, if using, in a small saucepan and heat gently until melted and runny. Brush the jam all over the tart filling with a pastry brush and leave for a few more minutes before serving. Alternatively, serve it chilled with cream or custard.

When peaches are in season and at their juicy best, the most simple of recipes are all that are required to bring out the best of the fruit. This rustic tart is so easy (you don't even need a pan) and so tasty. Or simply roast the peaches in the oven and serve them with lashings of indulgent mascarpone cheese. The vanilla sugar is easy to make—just put a couple of vanilla beans in a jar of sugar and leave them there, topping up with fresh sugar as necessary.

free-form caramelized peach tart

12 oz. ready-made puff pastry, defrosted if frozen

4–6 ripe peaches

5 tablespoons butter

freshly squeezed juice of ½ lemon

1 cup sugar

whipped cream or crème fraîche, to serve

a dinner plate, 11 inches diameter (to use as a template)

a baking sheet

serves 6

Preheat the oven to 450°F.

Roll out the pastry on a lightly floured work surface and cut out a circle, 11 inches diameter, using a large dinner plate as a template. Lift onto a baking sheet and make an edge by twisting the dough over itself all the way around the edge. Press lightly to seal. Still on the baking sheet, chill or freeze for at least 15 minutes.

Peel the peaches if necessary, then halve and pit them, and cut into chunky slices. Put the butter into a saucepan, then add the lemon juice and half the sugar. Heat until melted, then add the peaches and toss gently. Pile the peaches all over the dough in a casual way. Sprinkle with the remaining sugar, and bake in the preheated oven for 20–25 minutes until golden, puffed, and caramelized. Serve with whipped cream or crème fraîche.

roasted mascarpone peaches

4 large ripe peaches

2 tablespoons clear honey

5½ oz. mascarpone cheese

3 tablespoons vanilla sugar

1 tablespoon freshly squeezed lemon juice

serves 4

Cut the peaches in half, remove the pits, and arrange the fruit cut side up in a roasting pan. Pour over the honey and bake in a preheated oven at 400°F for about 20 minutes until softened and lightly golden.

Mix the mascarpone with the vanilla sugar and lemon juice and spoon onto the hot peaches. Serve at once.

If you have an abundance of juicy summer peaches, try these two recipes: a cake to enjoy straight away, and a jar of preserved fruit to store in the cupboard and bring out for a quick dessert, served with cream. You can use either yellow or white peaches here—the yellow varieties have a more robust flavor, while the white ones are more subtle. Peach halves in brandy are a classic, but all kinds of fruits can be preserved in this way: try nectarine halves, cherries, apricots, or plums (although these fruits will not need to be peeled) and substitute the star anise for a cinnamon stick or vanilla bean.

peach halves in brandy with star anise

4 firm just-ripe peaches
2 cups sugar
1 cup brandy
1 whole star anise

1 pint sterilized, sealable jar (see note on page 4)

makes 1 pint

Put the peaches in a large bowl and cover with boiling water. Leave for 2 minutes for the skins to lift, drain off the water, and pull off the skins. Discard the water. Cut the peaches in half and poach in plenty of simmering water for 1–2 minutes until just tender. Lift out the peach halves with a slotted spoon and drain on paper towels.

Measure 2 cups of the poaching water into a pan. Add 1½ cups of the sugar, dissolve over low heat, then bring to a boil and boil for 7 minutes. Don't forget to keep an eye on it.

When the peaches have cooled, arrange them in a heatproof dish in a single layer, cover with the boiling syrup and leave for 24 hours.

After this time, pour the syrup off the peach halves into a saucepan and add the remaining ½ cup sugar. Bring slowly to simmering point to dissolve the sugar, then boil for 2 minutes. Pour this back over the peaches, cool, cover with a cloth or lid, and leave for 2 more days. After 2 days, transfer the peach halves to a clean ½-quart jar.

Pour 1 cup of the syrup into a large measuring cup and add to it an equal quantity of brandy. Pour the mixture over the peaches until covered, add the star anise on the outside of the fruit but on the inside of the glass, and keep for at least 1 month before using.

upside-down peach cake

4 large peaches
1 stick unsalted butter, softened
1 scant cup brown sugar
3 eggs, separated
¾ cup plus 2 tablespoons self-rising flour

1 cup sour cream
confectioners' sugar, for dusting
light cream, to serve (optional)

a 9-inch diameter springform cake pan, base-lined with baking parchment and lightly greased

Preheat the oven to 350°F. Halve the peaches, discard the pit, then cut each half in half again. Arrange the peaches on the bottom of the cake pan and set aside while making the cake batter.

Put the butter and sugar in a large bowl and beat with an electric whisk until the sugar has completely dissolved and the mixture is the color of caramel. Add the egg yolks, 1 at a time, beating for 1 minute between each addition. Fold the flour and sour cream through in 2 batches.

In a separate grease-free bowl, beat the egg whites with an electric whisk until they form firm peaks. Using a large metal spoon, fold the whites into the cake batter in 2 batches. Spoon the batter over the peaches and bake in the preheated oven for 40–45 minutes, until the top of the cake is golden and the centre springs back when gently pressed.

Let cool in the pan for 10 minutes before carefully turning out onto a serving plate. Dust with confectioners' sugar and serve warm with light cream for pouring, if liked.

These two summery recipes are packed full of sweet, ripe produce. The nectarines in both recipes can be swapped for a similar quantity of peaches, plums, or apricots, to suit your crop. But whatever fruit you choose, the tray bake is best made and eaten on the same day. Crumbles are normally considered to be a comforting winter pudding, but this deliciously light, nutty version makes the most of juicy summer nectarines. It takes very little time to prepare and tastes sublime with ice cream.

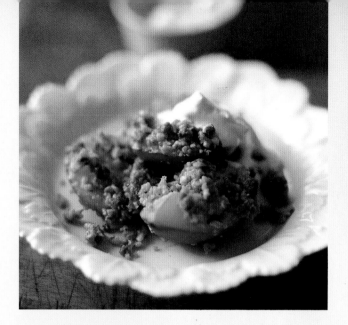

nectarine, blueberry, & lavender tray bake

3 large eggs

1 cup caster sugar

1¼ cups self-rising flour, sifted

1 teaspoon baking powder

½ teaspoon vanilla extract

1½ sticks butter, softened and cubed

½ tablespoon dried lavender buds

3 ripe but firm nectarines

1½ cup blueberries

1 tablespoon cornmeal

lavender sugar

½ tablespoon dried lavender buds

2 tablespoons sugar

grated zest of 1 lemon

a 9 x 13-inch baking pan, lined with baking parchment and lightly buttered

serves 14

Preheat the oven to 350°F.

Put the eggs, sugar, flour, baking powder, vanilla extract, butter, and lavender in an electric mixer (or use a mixing bowl and an electric whisk) and whisk together. Pit the nectarines, chop them into bite-sized pieces and stir into the mixture along with the blueberries.

Dust the bottom of the prepared pan with the cornmeal and a very small amount of flour. Spoon the batter into the pan and spread it evenly with a spatula.

To make the lavender sugar, mix all the ingredients together in a bowl, then scatter evenly over the batter.

Bake in the preheated oven for 35 minutes, or until risen and golden brown. Let cool in the pan before cutting into 14 rectangles.

nectarine & pistachio summer crumble

½ cup shelled pistachio nuts, coarsely chopped

⅓ cup blanched whole almonds

½ cup ground oatmeal

4 tablespoons cold unsalted butter, cubed

½ cup all-purpose flour

½ cup packed brown sugar

6 nectarines

vanilla ice cream or heavy cream, to serve

a baking sheet, lined with baking parchment

serves 6

To make the crumble topping, put the pistachios and almonds in a food processor and process until coarsely chopped. Transfer to a bowl. Add the oatmeal and butter and use your fingertips to rub the ingredients together until the mixture resembles coarse, wet sand. Add the flour and sugar and rub together to combine. Cover and refrigerate until needed.

Preheat the oven to 425°F.

Line a baking sheet with baking parchment. Cut the nectarines in half. If the pit does not come out easily, don't worry—simply slice the flesh off the fruit and drop it directly onto the baking sheet. Sprinkle the crumble topping evenly over the nectarines and bake in the preheated oven for 10–15 minutes, until the fruit is soft and juicy and the topping is a soft golden color. Serve warm with ice cream or heavy cream.

The word slump perfectly describes the sloppy batter which covers the seasonal fruit in this satisfying dessert. Normally the fruit is on the bottom and the thick batter spooned or poured roughly over the top, but this recipe celebrates the fruit, so pour the batter in first, then push in the apricots. You can use any juicy fruit and berries are really good too. The apricot betty is another wonderful, old-fashioned fruit dessert. If you have the patience, you can crack the apricot kernels and take out the nuts inside. These are very like bitter almonds, and are a fantastic addition when chopped and toasted with the breadcrumbs.

buttered apricot betty

1½ lbs. fresh apricots

1 stick unsalted butter, cubed

3 cups fresh breadcrumbs, lightly toasted

2 tablespoons golden syrup

⅓ cup orange juice

¼ cup superfine sugar

a medium, ovenproof, deep pie or soufflé dish

a large roasting pan

serves 4

Preheat the oven to 375°F.

Halve the fresh apricots and remove the pits. Butter a deep pie or soufflé dish and place a layer of apricots on the base.

Reserve 4–6 tablespoons of breadcrumbs for the top. Sprinkle some of the rest of the breadcrumbs over the apricots, and dot with some of the butter. Put in some more apricots and repeat these alternate casual layers until all the apricots and breadcrumbs are used up. Use the reserved breadcrumbs for the final top layer.

Warm the syrup with the orange juice, and pour this over the top. Sprinkle with sugar and dot with the remaining butter.

Place the pie dish in a roasting pan and pour in enough boiling water to come halfway up the sides of the dish. Bake in the preheated oven for 45 minutes, or until the apricots are soft and the top crispy and golden brown. Serve warm, not hot, with cream.

apricot & almond slump

1½ lbs. fresh apricots

¾ cup light brown sugar

almond slump batter

1½ cups all-purpose flour

3 teaspoons baking powder

a pinch of salt

1 cup ground almonds

about 1½ cups whole milk

4 tablespoons unsalted butter, melted

¼ cup whole blanched almonds

a large, non-stick, metal baking pan, greased

serves 4–6

Preheat the oven to 375°F.

Halve the apricots, remove the pits, and mix with ½ cup of the sugar. Set aside until needed.

Sift together the flour, baking powder, salt, and remaining sugar into a bowl. Stir in the ground almonds, milk, and melted butter and whisk until smooth and thick. Pour the batter into the baking pan, then push in the apricots cut side up, but in a higgledy-piggledy manner and slightly at an angle all over. Place a whole almond inside each apricot where the pit once was.

Bake the slump for 25–30 minutes in the middle of the preheated oven, until risen and golden.

Remove from the oven and allow to cool slightly before serving with vanilla ice cream.

white chocolate & apricot roulade

This summer stunner, once assembled, will hold for a couple of hours before serving—keep it in a cool place, but not the refrigerator. To make it look extra special, use a vegetable peeler to make curls from a block of white chocolate to scatter on top.

Preheat the oven to 375°F.

Break the eggs into a large heatproof mixing bowl and add the sugar and saffron. Place over a pan of simmering water, making sure the base doesn't touch the water. Using an electric whisk, whisk the ingredients for 5 minutes, or until pale and voluminous. Take the bowl off the heat. Using a large metal spoon, carefully fold the flour into the mixture.

Tip the mixture into the prepared pan and gently spread it evenly with a spatula. Sprinkle the slivered almonds over the top. Bake in the preheated oven for 12–15 minutes, or until lightly golden. Meanwhile, cover a large board with a sheet of baking parchment and sift the tablespoon of confectioners' sugar evenly over it.

When the cake is ready, let it set, out of the oven, for 10 minutes. Run a small, sharp knife around the edges before turning it upside down over the sugared baking parchment. Remove the pan and peel off the parchment paper. Roll up the cake from one of the shorter ends, rolling the sugared baking parchment with it as you do so—you may need to make a cut along the width of the cake, about an inch in, to help you start rolling. Once rolled, leave the cake to cool completely.

To make the apricot filling, put all the ingredients in a pan and simmer gently, uncovered, for 10 minutes—you want the apricots to be soft, but still retain their shape. Leave to cool, then refrigerate until needed.

To make the white chocolate cream, put the chocolate pieces and 2 tablespoons of the crème fraîche in a small heatproof bowl over a pan of barely simmering water. Leave until melted, stirring from time to time. Take the bowl off the heat and let cool slightly. Whisk the cream in a bowl until it forms soft peaks, then stir in the remaining crème fraîche and the cooled chocolate mixture.

Unroll the cake onto a large board. Spread the white chocolate cream over it and scatter the apricot mixture on top. Roll up the roulade and dust with confectioners' sugar.

4 large eggs
½ cup sugar
2 pinches of saffron threads
¾ cup self-rising flour, sifted
3 tablespoons slivered almonds
1 tablespoon confectioners' sugar, plus extra for dusting

apricot filling

seeds from 4 cardamom pods, crushed

1 tablespoon honey, preferably orange blossom

1 tablespoon freshly squeezed lemon juice

8 apricots, pitted and finely chopped

white chocolate cream

2½ oz. white chocolate, broken into pieces, plus extra if making curls

⅔ cup crème fraîche

¾ cup heavy cream

a 9 x 14-inch jelly roll pan, 1 inch deep, oiled and base-lined with baking parchment

serves 10–12

apricots   **163**

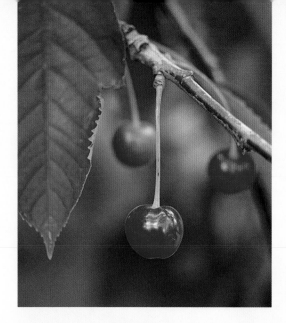

This is such a pretty option for a summer afternoon tea in the garden, but it can also be adapted to whatever seasonal fruits are available. Strawberries and raspberries make a nice topping with a little shredded lemon verbena, or try thin slices of baked quince, a handful of blackberries, and a scattering of toasted nuts for a wonderful fall variation.

cherry, peach, & vanilla shortcake

¾ cup all-purpose flour

5 tablespoons butter, softened and cubed

¼ cup confectioners' sugar, sifted

1 egg yolk

topping

1 vanilla bean, split lengthwise

½ cup heavy or whipping cream, chilled

2 tablespoons confectioners' sugar, plus extra for dusting

2 ripe but firm peaches, pitted and sliced

1 cup cherries, pitted and halved

a squeeze of lemon juice

2 tablespoons freshly shredded basil leaves

a baking sheet, lined with baking parchment

serves 4

Put the flour, butter, sugar, and egg yolk in a food processor and mix together. If the dough doesn't come together, tip it into a bowl and work it with a spatula. Alternatively, you can make it by hand to start with. Tip the dough onto a lightly floured work surface and bring it together in a ball. Press the ball into a disc, wrap in plastic wrap, and refrigerate for 15 minutes.

Preheat the oven to 375°F.

Tip the dough out onto the lightly floured work surface and roll or pat it out until it is big enough to cut out a 6-inch round—you can use a plate or upturned bowl to cut around.

Transfer the round to the prepared baking sheet and bake in the preheated oven for 10–12 minutes, or until set and lightly golden at the edges. Let cool completely.

To make the topping, scrape the seeds out of the vanilla bean into a bowl with the cream and half the confectioners' sugar. Whip into soft peaks.

Toss the sliced peaches and halved cherries with the lemon juice, basil, and the remaining confectioners' sugar.

Dust the cold shortcake lightly with more confectioners' sugar, then top with the cream mixture and scatter the fruit mixture over the top. Serve immediately.

Who said summer cooking couldn't include comfort food? These hearty baked desserts include a classic French clafoutis, and a modern take on a retro strudel. Fresh ricotta cheese is combined with ripe cherries and crispy phyllo with great success.

cherry & ricotta strudel

1 lb. fresh cherries, pitted

⅓ cup confectioners' sugar, plus extra for dusting

2 teaspoons cornstarch

⅔ cup ground almonds*

5 oz. fresh ricotta cheese

8 sheets of phyllo pastry, thawed if frozen

5 tablespoons unsalted butter, melted

serves 8

Put the cherries, 1 tablespoon of the confectioners' sugar, and the cornstarch in a bowl and let sit for 30 minutes, stirring often. Preheat the oven to 425°F.

Put the ground almonds and 2 tablepoons of the remaining confectioners' sugar in a bowl and mix to combine. Put the ricotta in a separate bowl, add the remaining confectioners' sugar and mix to combine. Set aside until needed. Put a baking sheet in the preheated oven to heat up. (This will prevent the bottom layer of phyllo becoming soggy.)

Put a sheet of baking parchment on a work surface. Lay a sheet of phyllo on the baking parchment, longest edge nearest to you. Brush all over with melted butter until the phyllo is shiny. Sprinkle 1–2 tablespoons of the ground almond mixture over the pastry. Repeat with the remaining sheets of phyllo, butter, and almond mixture, finishing with the final sheet of phyllo.

Working quickly, so that the phyllo does not become soggy, spread the ricotta mixture over the pastry, leaving a 2-inch margin around the edges. Spoon the cherry mixture over the top. Fold the edge nearest to you up and over the filling, tucking in the shorter edges as you roll. Make sure the strudel is sitting seam-side down. Use the baking parchment to lift the strudel onto the hot baking sheet. Bake in the preheated oven for 12–15 minutes, until lightly golden.

Remove and allow to cool slightly before dusting with confectioners' sugar and cutting into slices to serve.

*Note You can buy pre-packed ground almonds, or grind your own. It only takes a few minutes and the difference in fuller, richer flavor is well worth it. Simply put them on a baking sheet and toast them in an oven preheated to 350°F for 5 minutes. Allow them to cool and then process them in a food processor.

cherry & almond clafoutis

1 cup blanched almonds

1 vanilla bean (optional)

3 tablespoons all-purpose flour

1¼ cups sugar

4 eggs

2 egg yolks

1 cup light cream

8 oz. cherries, torn in half and pitted

a round ovenproof dish, 8–9 inches diameter

serves 4

Preheat the oven to 425°F.

Put the almonds on a baking sheet and toast them in the preheated oven for 6–8 minutes, until lightly golden. Remove and let cool. Put the cooled almonds in a food processor. Scrape the seeds from the vanilla bean into the food processor with the almonds and process until the mixture resembles a coarse meal. Add the flour and sugar and process to mix. Add the eggs, egg yolks, and cream, and process again until you have a smooth, thick batter. Transfer to a bowl, cover, and refrigerate until needed—it will keep for 2 days in the refrigerator.

Put the torn cherry halves in the bottom of an ovenproof dish. Carefully pour the batter over the cherries. If need be, rearrange the cherries to evenly distribute. (If using refrigerated batter, beat it until well mixed before pouring over the cherries.)

Cook in the preheated oven for 25 minutes, until the clafoutis is puffed up and golden brown. Allow to cool for a few minutes before serving. The clafoutis will sink during this time. Serve the clafoutis hot with vanilla ice cream.

italian fig conserve

3 lbs. firm black figs
freshly squeezed juice
of 2 lemons
6 cups sugar
½ tablespoon pure vanilla
extract

3–4 sealable, sterilized jars
(see note on page 4)
waxed paper discs

makes about 1 quart

Although ripe figs are delicious enjoyed as they are, cooking them really brings out the sweetness. To make this delicious fig conserve, make sure you use only plump, firm fruit. You can use green figs, but they should be peeled first. It is perfect with crusty bread and butter, brioche, or toast for breakfast, but would also make excellent jam tartlets.

* tip

This is a simple method for testing the setting point of jam without the aid of a sugar thermometer. As the jam boils it will start to become thicker and more syrupy. At this point, take it off the heat and put a teaspoonful on a saucer that you have chilled in the fridge. Leave for 5 minutes, then push the surface of the jam with your finger—if it wrinkles, the jam has reached setting point, otherwise return to the heat and boil again, testing at 4–5 minute intervals.

Wipe the figs and chop into tiny pieces. Put in a saucepan with the lemon juice and 1 scant cup water. Cook over low heat until soft —this may take 20–30 minutes, but if the skins are not cooked until tender at this stage, they will be tough when boiled with the sugar. Add the sugar and cook over low heat until dissolved. Stir in the vanilla sugar, increase the heat, and boil until setting point is reached, about 5–10 minutes.

Take the pan off the heat and test for set. If the jam is not ready, put the pan back on the heat to boil for a few minutes longer and test again. Repeat this process if necessary and remember to take the jam off the heat while testing, because over-boiling will ruin it.

When the jam has reached setting point, skim it with a perforated skimmer, stir it well, and let stand for 20 minutes for the fruit to settle. Stir and ladle into clean, dry, warm jars. Seal at once with waxed paper discs, wiping the necks of the jars with a clean, damp cloth if necessary. Close with a lid or appropriate cover. Leave to cool, label, and store in a cool, dark cupboard until required.

Variation Try experimenting with peaches, nectarines, and kiwifruit, though it may not be necessary to cook the fruit for so long.

Muscat is a grape variety that produces deliciously sweet and syrupy dessert wines known as moscato in Italy and moscatel in Spain. Whichever one you choose, the result will be the same—a fragrant and light dessert that is guaranteed to delight.

spiced muscat figs

1 cup muscat (sweet dessert wine)

⅔ cup superfine sugar

1 vanilla bean

2 cardamom pods, lightly crushed

2 strips of orange zest

8 fresh green figs

serves 4

Put the muscat, sugar, vanilla, cardamom pods, and orange zest in a medium saucepan and set over high heat. Bring the mixture to a boil, then reduce the heat to medium. Add the figs to the pan, cover, and cook for 20–25 minutes, until the figs are very tender. Remove the figs from the pan with a slotted spoon and set aside.

Return the liquid to a boil and cook for 8–10 minutes, until thick and syrupy.

Serve 2 figs per person, with the syrup spooned over the top.

soft fruits

strawberry tiramisú ❦ pink cava & strawberry jellies
strawberry buttermilk cake ❦ summer fruit &
white chocolate muffins ❦ strawberry jam
strawberries with black pepper ❦ chocolate-dipped
strawberries ❦ strawberry eton mess
fresh raspberry & almond tart ❦ little raspberry &
rose cobblers ❦ uncooked freezer raspberry jam
raspberry cream ❦ blackberry crumble
baked brioche pudding with blackberries
baked blueberry & granny smith pudding
cinnamon blueberry cake ❦ rhubarb clafoutis
rhubarb, strawberry, & rose fool
rhubarb custard & crumble tartlets

Here are two fruity desserts that are sure to delight guests at a summer garden party. A sumptuous Italian classic has been given a summer makeover with the inclusion of freshly picked strawberries. And, on the lighter side, pink cava and strawberry jellies make a delicate, pretty dessert. Adding a dash of strawberry-flavored syrup or liqueur to the liquid jelly will make this even more delicious.

strawberry tiramisù

14 oz. fresh ripe strawberries

5 hard amaretti cookies

2 large eggs, separated

3 tablespoons superfine sugar

¼ teaspoon pure vanilla extract

4 tablespoons white rum

8 oz. mascarpone cheese, at room temperature

3 tablespoons whipping cream

6 tablespoons apple juice

3 oz. savoiardi (ladyfinger cookies)

a medium–large, deep, glass dessert bowl

serves 6

Hull the strawberries. Measure out ½ cup and chop them finely. Slice the remaining strawberries and set aside. Put the amaretti biscuits in a plastic bag, seal, then hit them with a rolling pin until they are the consistency of coarse breadcrumbs.

Beat the egg yolks in a bowl with an electric handheld whisk until pale yellow and fluffy, gradually adding the sugar as you go. Add the vanilla extract and a tablespoon of the white rum. Tip the mascarpone cheese into a large bowl, beat with a wooden spoon to soften, then gradually add the egg yolk mixture and beat until smooth. In another bowl, whisk the egg whites until they just hold a soft peak. Fold the chopped strawberries into the mascarpone cheese mixture, then carefully fold in the egg whites.

Whip the cream to a similar consistency then fold that in too, along with a third of the crushed amaretti biscuits. Mix the remaining rum with the apple juice. Dip some of the savoiardi in the apple-rum mixture and lay across the base of your bowl. Reserving some sliced strawberries for decoration, arrange a layer of strawberries over the biscuits, then cover with a layer of mascarpone cream. Repeat with 1 or 2 more layers of soaked biscuits, strawberries and mascarpone cream, finishing with the mascarpone cream. Cover the bowl tightly with plastic wrap and chill for at least 5 hours.

About 1 hour before serving, sprinkle the remaining amaretti biscuits over the top of the tiramisù, then decorate with the remaining strawberries. Return the tiramisù to the refrigerator until you are ready to serve it.

pink cava & strawberry jellies

12 sheets of gelatin (or enough to set 5 cups of liquid)

5 cups Cava Rosado or other sparkling rosé

1¾ lbs. fresh strawberries

2–3 tablespoons sugar, depending on how ripe your strawberries are

⅓–½ cup homemade sugar syrup* or store-bought gomme

cream or vanilla ice cream, to serve

12 wine glasses or small glass serving dishes

serves 12

Lay the gelatin in a large flat dish and sprinkle over 6 tablespoons cold water. Leave to soak for 3 minutes until soft. Heat the wine in a microwave or saucepan until hot but not boiling. Tip the soaked gelatine into the wine and stir to dissolve, then set aside to cool.

Rinse the strawberries and cut them into halves or quarters to give even-sized pieces. Put them into a shallow bowl, sprinkle over the sugar, and leave them to macerate. Check the liquid jelly for sweetness, adding the sugar syrup to taste. Divide half the strawberries between 12 glasses or glass dishes then pour over enough jelly to cover them. Put in the fridge to chill. As soon as the jelly has set (about an hour), add the rest of the fruit and jelly. Return to the fridge to set for another 45 minutes–1 hour before serving with cream or ice cream.

*Note To make the sugar syrup, dissolve ½ cup sugar in ½ cup water. Heat gently together in a pan. When all the grains are dissolved, bring to a boil and simmer for 2–3 minutes. Use it immediately or cool and store it for up to two weeks in the refrigerator.

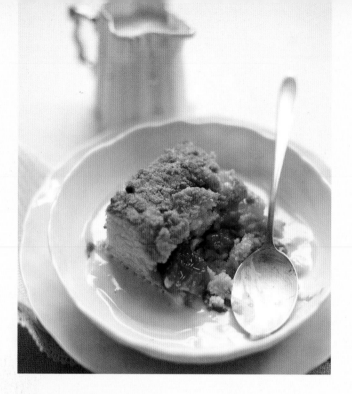

Sweet summer strawberries are so good you will want to eat a whole bowl on their own. Although strawberries are a fruit that are best appreciated raw, occasionally you will come across great recipes to the contrary, like these two: a smooth, dense cake given a light and creamy crumb by using buttermilk, or moist muffins packed full of fruit and nuggets of white chocolate. Both are a truly indulgent treat.

summer fruit & white chocolate muffins

2 eggs

5 tablespoons sugar

3 tablespoons vegetable oil (or groundnut or safflower)

a few drops of vanilla extract

1 cup plus 3 tablespoons all-purpose flour

1½ teaspoons baking powder

1 large nectarine, pitted and sliced

½ cup strawberries, hulled and quartered

2½ oz. white chocolate, chopped

topping

½ nectarine, pitted and sliced

½ cup raspberries

3 strawberries, hulled and quartered

light brown sugar, to sprinkle

a muffin pan, lined with 6 muffin cases

makes 6

Preheat the oven to 350°F.

Put the eggs, sugar, oil, and vanilla in a mixing bowl and mix well until you have a smooth liquid. Mix the flour and baking powder together in a separate bowl, then mix into the wet ingredients. Stir in the nectarines, strawberries, and chocolate until evenly mixed.

Fill each muffin case about two-thirds full with batter. Scatter the fruit for the topping over the muffins and finish with a sprinkling of sugar. Bake in the preheated oven for about 25 minutes. Do not be tempted to open the oven door halfway through baking as it might cause the muffins to sink. When they are ready, they should be well risen and springy to the touch.

Muffins are always best eaten warm from the oven, but if you have some left over you can always refresh them with a quick flash in the microwave. Store in an airtight container for 2–3 days.

strawberry buttermilk cake

2 cups self-rising flour

1 cup plus 2 tablespoons sugar

1 stick unsalted butter, softened

2 eggs

1 cup buttermilk

12 oz. strawberries, hulled, large ones halved

vanilla custard or heavy cream, to serve

crumble topping

5 tablespoons all-purpose flour

½ stick unsalted butter, chilled and cubed

½ cup packed brown sugar

an 8 inch x 8 inch cake pan, greased and lined

serves 6–8

Preheat the oven to 350°F.

Put the flour and sugar in a bowl and mix. Put the butter, eggs, and buttermilk in a food processor and process until smooth and combined. With the motor running, add the flour and sugar and process until well mixed. Scrape down the sides of the bowl to evenly incorporate all the ingredients. Transfer the mixture to a bowl and stir in the strawberries. Spoon the batter into the lined cake pan.

To make the crumble topping, put the flour and butter in a bowl and, using the tips of your fingers, rub the butter into the flour until the mixture resembles coarse breadcrumbs. Stir in the sugar.

Evenly sprinkle the topping mixture over the cake and bake in the preheated oven for 50 minutes, until golden brown on top.

Leave to cool before cutting into slices or squares and serving with vanilla custard or a dollop of heavy cream.

strawberry jam

2 lbs. slightly under-ripe strawberries, hulled and halved

3¾ cups preserving or granulated sugar

freshly squeezed juice of 1 lemon

1 tablespoon butter

2 x ½ pint sealable, sterilized jars (see note on page 4)

waxed paper discs

makes 2 x ½ pint jars

Put the strawberries and sugar in a large non-metal bowl. Cover and leave to macerate overnight.

The next day, transfer the strawberries and sugar to a large preserving pan or non-aluminum saucepan and set over very low heat to dissolve any remaining sugar. Add the lemon juice and bring to a boil. Cook for 8–25 minutes, depending on the water content of the strawberries, or until setting point has been reached (see page 166).

Stir in the butter to disperse any scum. Leave to cool for about 20 minutes, then transfer to the sterilized jars (wiping off any drips). Cover with waxed discs and seal with the lids whilst still warm. Label with the date and store in a cool, dark place for up to 6 months.

strawberries with black pepper

1 lb. strawberries

1 tablespoon orange flower water (optional)

1 tablespoon sugar

2 teaspoons cracked black pepper

serves 4

Hull the strawberries and cut in half. Sprinkle with the orange flower water, if using, and with the sugar and black pepper. Chill for 15 minutes and serve.

Note Strawberries should be washed and dried before hulling, not after, otherwise they fill up with water.

chocolate-dipped strawberries

3½ oz. dark chocolate

3½ oz. white chocolate

12 large strawberries

baking parchment

12 wooden skewers

serves 12

Put the chocolate into 2 separate bowls and set the bowls over 2 saucepans of simmering water. When melted, dip the pointed end of each strawberry into one of the chocolates and transfer to the sheet of baking parchment. When set, slide each strawberry onto a skewer and serve.

strawberry eton mess

1¼ cups heavy (or whipping) cream

7 oz. thick Greek yogurt

6 plain meringues or meringue shells

16 ripe, juicy strawberries, halved

serves 4–6

Put the cream into a large bowl whisk until it makes soft peaks. Don't over-whisk otherwise the cream will be too firm. Add the yogurt and gently fold everything together.

Over another bowl, gently crush the meringues with your fingers to break into small pieces. Add the meringue and strawberries to the cream mixture and gently mix together.

Spoon the mixture into small serving bowls and put in the fridge for 20 minutes before you serve.

If you have an abundance of raspberries, they freeze really well and can be used in future dishes. These two recipes use frozen raspberries, as they are often easier to work with when a little less mushy. The raspberry and almond tart tastes better the day after it's made, which makes it ideal for preparing ahead of any guests arriving for a summer afternoon tea!

fresh raspberry & almond tart

1 egg

3 tablespoons sugar

1 tablespoon all-purpose flour

5 tablespoons unsalted butter

5 oz. fresh raspberries, frozen until firm

chilled light cream, to serve (optional)

almond shortcrust pastry

⅓ cup ground almonds

1½ cups all-purpose flour

7 tablespoons sugar

1 stick unsalted butter, chilled and cubed

a rectangular tart pan, 5 x 8 inches, lightly greased

serves 6–8

Preheat the oven to 350°F.

To make the pastry, put the ground almonds, flour, and sugar in a food processor. With the motor running, add a cube of butter at a time until it is all incorporated and the mixture resembles coarse breadcrumbs. Add 2 tablespoons cold water and process until just combined. Be careful not to overprocess.

Tip the dough out onto a lightly-floured work surface and knead to form a ball. Roll it out between 2 layers of baking parchment until it is about 2 inches longer and 2 inches wider than the tart pan. Carefully lift the dough into the pan and use your fingers to press it down into the base and sides, letting it overhang. Prick the base all over with a fork and bake in the preheated oven for 20 minutes, until lightly golden. Break off the overhanging pastry.

Put the egg, sugar, and flour in a bowl and use a balloon whisk to beat until thick and pale. Put the butter in a small saucepan and set over medium heat. Let melt until frothy and dark golden with a nutty aroma. Working quickly, pour the melted butter over the egg mixture and beat well. Scatter the raspberries in the tart crust. Pour the warm batter over the raspberries. Bake in the still-hot oven for about 45 minutes, until the top resembles a golden meringue. Let cool for 30 minutes before serving. Cut into slices and serve with chilled cream, if liked.

little raspberry & rose cobblers

1⅓ lbs. fresh raspberries, half of them frozen

for the cobbler bases

petals of 2 pink or red roses, washed and dried (optional)

½ stick unsalted butter, chilled

1¾ cups self-rising flour

a pinch of salt

¼ sugar (vanilla flavored if available)

1 tablespoon rosewater extract

about ⅔ cup whole milk

confectioners' sugar, to dust

heavy cream, to serve

a non-stick, four-hole muffin pan

serves 4

Preheat the oven to 425°F.

Select the most attractive rose petals and put these to one side to use as decoration. Shred the remaining ones. Rub the butter into the flour and salt until it resembles fine breadcrumbs. Stir the sugar and shredded rose petals into this mixture.

Stir the rosewater into the milk and pour into the flour, mixing with a blunt knife to a fairly soft, sticky dough. Tip out onto a flour-dusted work surface and roll out until ½ inch thick. Cut out 4 rounds (approximately 6 inches wide) that will fill a four-cup muffin pan.

Place the rounds gently in the pan and carefully push the frozen raspberries into the dough. Dust with confectioners' sugar and bake for 10–15 minutes, until the dough is risen and golden brown. Remove from the oven.

Carefully lift the cobblers out of the pan and serve warm with the remaining fresh raspberries, a scattering of rose petals, a dusting of confectioners' sugar, and a pitcher of heavy cream.

raspberries 179

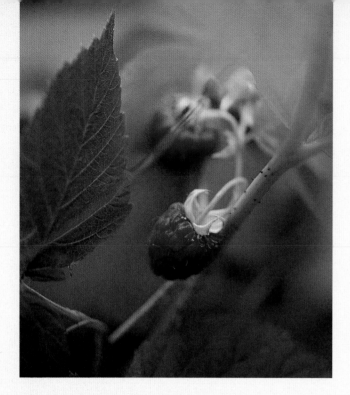

Raspberry jam, made from the freshest, sweetest fruit, and served on hot, buttered toast, really cannot be beaten for pure pleasure. And there is no boiling needed in this recipe so not only is it simple to make, you keep all the taste of the fruit, too. Commercially produced "jam sugar" is perfect for this—it has added pectin that helps the preserve thicken to a soft set. Use ½ cup liquid pectin if you can't find this special jam sugar. More indulgence comes in the form of this classic French raspberry cream, although you can vary the fruit to what you have available—try it with strawberries or a mixture of summer berries.

uncooked freezer raspberry jam

1¾ lbs. fresh raspberries

5 cups sugar with added pectin (sometimes known as "jam sugar")

2 tablespoons freshly squeezed lemon juice

makes 2 x 16-oz. pots

Tip the raspberries into a bowl and crush a little with a potato masher. Stir in the jam sugar and lemon juice. Cover with plastic wrap and heat on "medium" in the microwave for about 5 minutes or until warmed through.

Uncover and stir gently to dissolve the sugar, then leave to stand overnight. Alternatively, heat in a saucepan until the sugar has dissolved.

The next day, pot up into freezer containers and freeze—keep one pot in the refrigerator for breakfast tomorrow. After removing from the freezer, store the jam in the refrigerator. Thaw before using.

raspberry cream

12 oz. raspberries, fresh or frozen and thawed plus 1 small basket of fresh raspberries

5–6 tablespoons sugar, to taste

1 cup whipping cream, chilled

1 large egg white

sprigs of fresh mint, to serve

serves 4

Put the raspberries in a blender or food processor and blend until smooth, then press through a sieve to obtain a smooth purée; you should have about 1 cup. Stir in 4–5 tablespoons of the sugar. Set aside.

Put the cream in a large bowl and whisk with an electric mixer until it holds firm peaks. Set aside.

Whisk the egg white with 1 tablespoon of the sugar until it holds firm peaks. Fold the beaten egg white and raspberry purée into the cream.

Divide the mixture between 4 serving glasses, filling half-way. Set aside 4 fresh raspberries, then divide the remaining fresh ones between the glasses and top with the remaining raspberry cream.

Decorate the top of each with a fresh raspberry and a mint sprig. Chill for up to 6 hours. Serve cold.

Variation Use fromage frais in place of the whipped cream, or use half whipped cream and half fromage frais. This can also be made with strawberries or mixed berries, though you will have to adjust the sugar content. Sweeten the fruit purée gradually, tasting as you go, until it is to your liking.

There is nothing so comforting as a baked fruit dessert served with thick cream or a rich custard. A blackberry crumble is the most classic of desserts, but this impressive but simple brioche pudding is also well worth a try. The sweet and buttery brioche works well with the tangy blackberries and the dark purple juices should bleed into the pudding to create a pretty, marbled effect. Try and pick very sweet blackberries for both of these recipes, as they will be softer and juicier.

blackberry crumble

12 oz. blackberries
1 tablespoon granulated sugar
1 teaspoon cornstarch
1 cup all-purpose flour
5 tablespoons unsalted butter, cubed and chilled

¼ cup packed light brown sugar
heavy cream, to serve
a medium ovenproof dish, lightly buttered

serves 4

Preheat the oven to 350°F.

Put the blackberries in a bowl with the granulated sugar and the cornstarch and toss to mix. Tumble the berries into the buttered baking dish and set aside for 15–20 minutes.

Put the all-purpose flour and butter in a large bowl and, using the tips of your fingers, rub the butter into the flour until the mixture resembles coarse breadcrumbs. Stir in the brown sugar.

Sprinkle the mixture evenly over the berries and bake in the preheated oven for 45–50 minutes, until the top is golden brown.

Let the crumble cool slightly before serving with dollops of cream spooned on top.

* tip

The floral aroma of blackberries can be enhanced by adding a small splash of Middle Eastern rosewater or orange blossom essence to the berries. Keep this in mind whenever you are serving or cooking with blackberries or any red berry.

baked brioche pudding with blackberries

4 brioche rolls or ½ 14-oz. brioche loaf
3 tablespoons butter, softened
3 eggs
2 cups fresh blackberries
½ cup light cream
1½ cups whole milk

⅓ cup superfine sugar
2 tablespoons raw (unrefined) sugar
vanilla ice cream, to serve (optional)

serves 6

Slice the brioche to give you 6–8 thin slices. Lightly butter the slices on one side and arrange them in the bottom of a medium baking dish, overlapping them slightly. Put half the blackberries on top. Repeat with the remaining brioche slices and blackberries. Put the cream, eggs, milk, and superfine sugar in a bowl or pitcher and beat to combine. Pour the mixture over the brioche in the baking dish. Cover with foil and let sit for 30 minutes to allow the brioche to absorb the liquid.

Preheat the oven to 350°F. Sprinkle the raw sugar over the top of the pudding and bake it in the preheated oven for 40–45 minutes, until the top of the pudding is golden. Serve warm with vanilla ice cream, if liked.

baked blueberry & granny smith pudding

2 tart green apples, such as Granny Smith

1 cup blueberries

1 cup all-purpose flour

3 teaspoons baking powder

½ cup plus 2 tablespoons superfine sugar

1 cup buttermilk

1 egg

1 vanilla bean

½ cup packed light brown sugar

light cream, to serve (optional)

serves 6

Preheat the oven to 350°F.

Generously butter a medium baking dish. Peel and core the apples then thinly slice them directly into the baking dish, arranging them in the bottom of the dish with the blueberries.

Sift the flour, baking powder, and superfine sugar into a large bowl. Put the buttermilk and egg in a separate bowl. Split the vanilla bean in half lengthwise and scrape the seeds from the bean directly into this bowl, then stir to combine. Pour the buttermilk mixture into the flour mixture and beat well to combine.

Pour the mixture over the fruit in the baking dish. Working quickly, put the brown sugar in a pitcher and add 1 cup boiling water. Stir until the sugar has dissolved. Carefully pour this mixture into the baking dish, pouring into a corner. Bake the pudding in the preheated oven for 45 minutes, until the surface feels dry and springs back when lightly touched. Serve warm with cream for pouring, if liked.

Sweet, mild blueberries are a delicious partner to tangy apples. Granny Smiths are a good all-round cooking apple as their flesh collapses when cooked, making them perfect for sweet puddings. Or use fresh blueberries to make this spectacular-looking cake. Bake it on the day you are going to eat it, but let it cool completely before assembling and serving.

cinnamon blueberry cake

1½ sticks unsalted butter, softened

¾ cup sugar

4 large eggs, lightly beaten

a pinch of ground cinnamon

1⅓ cups self-rising flour, sifted

2 teaspoons baking powder

a pinch of salt

8 oz. blueberries

cinnamon frosting

6½ oz. cream cheese, chilled

a scant ½ cup crème fraîche or heavy cream, chilled

3 tablespoons unsalted butter, softened and cubed

1 cup confectioners' sugar, sifted, plus a little extra for dusting

2 teaspoons ground cinnamon

two 8-inch round cake pans, lightly buttered and base-lined with baking parchment

serves 8

Preheat the oven to 350°F.

Put the butter and sugar in an electric mixer (or use a large mixing bowl and an electric whisk) and beat for 3–4 minutes, or until pale and fluffy. Gradually add the beaten eggs with the beaters still running, followed by the cinnamon, flour, baking powder, and salt. Mix until all the ingredients are combined.

Divide the batter between the prepared pans and spread it evenly with a spatula. Bake in the preheated oven for 20–25 minutes, or until lightly golden brown and risen. Let cool in the pans for 30 minutes. Tip the cakes out onto a wire rack and peel off the parchment papers. Let cool completely.

To make the cinnamon frosting, whisk all the ingredients together to combine.

To assemble, place one cake on a cake stand or large serving plate and spread two-thirds of the cinnamon frosting over the top— a spatula or table knife is the ideal tool to use here. Scatter three-quarters of the blueberries on top of the frosting.

Place the other cake on the blueberries and spread the remaining frosting over the top. Finish with the rest of the blueberries. Dust with a little confectioners' sugar.

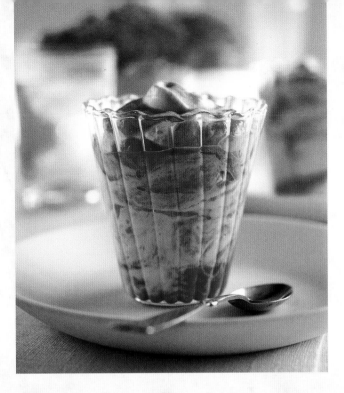

Clafoutis, a custard-like batter baked with whole cherries, is a speciality of the Limousin region. It is one of the finest French desserts and easy to make. The only drawback is that the cherry season is a short one. Plums, pears, and apples work well as substitutes, but rhubarb is fantastic, almost better than the original. Rhubarb is also a classic ingredient of the fruit fool, combined here with strawberries too. These two fruits have an extraordinary affinity, which is fortunate as they come into season at the same time of year.

rhubarb clafoutis

1 lb. fresh rhubarb, cut into 1-inch slices

¾ cup whole milk

¾ cup heavy cream

3 eggs

¾ cup sugar

¼ teaspoon ground cinnamon

a pinch of salt

1 vanilla bean, split lengthwise with a small sharp knife

⅓ cup all-purpose flour

a baking dish, about 12 inches diameter, greased with butter and sprinkled with sugar

serves 6

Bring a large saucepan of water to a boil, add the rhubarb, and cook for 2 minutes, just to blanch. Drain and set aside.

Put the milk, cream, eggs, sugar, cinnamon, and salt in a bowl and mix well. Using the tip of the knife, scrape the vanilla seeds into the mixture. Add the flour and whisk well.

Preheat the oven to 400°F.

Arrange the rhubarb in the prepared baking dish. Pour the batter over the top and bake in the preheated oven for 40–45 minutes, until puffed and golden.

rhubarb, strawberry, & rose fool

14 oz. fresh rhubarb

3 tablespoons superfine sugar

11½ oz. fresh, ripe strawberries, plus a few extra to garnish

2–3 tablespoons rose syrup or rosewater and extra superfine sugar

1¼ cups Greek yogurt

1¼ cups whipping cream

6 glasses or glass serving dishes

serves 6

Slice the rhubarb and put it in a saucepan with the sugar and 2 tablespoons water. Put a lid on the pan and heat over low heat until the fruit comes to a boil, then turn the heat down and simmer for 7–10 minutes until the fruit is soft. Tip the fruit into a sieve over a bowl and drain off the juice.

Hull the strawberries, put 8 oz. of them in a food processor and whizz until smooth. Add the drained rhubarb and 1 tablespoon rose syrup or 2 teaspoons rosewater with 1 tablespoon superfine sugar and whizz again. Tip the purée into a bowl and leave to cool. Tip the yogurt into a large bowl. In a separate bowl, whip the cream until just holding its shape and sweeten to taste with rose syrup or rosewater and sugar. Fold half the cream into the yogurt. Fold half the puréed strawberry and rhubarb into the yogurt and cream mixture then lightly mix the remaining cream and the rest of the rhubarb and strawberry purée to create a marbled effect.

Spoon the fool into individual glasses and chill until ready to serve. Slice the remaining strawberries and sprinkle with a few drops of rose syrup or a little sugar. Use the strawberry slices to decorate the top of each glass.

rhubarb custard
& crumble tartlets

pastry

2 cups all-purpose flour

1 stick unsalted butter, chilled and cubed

5 tablespoons sugar

1 egg

crumble

¾ cup all-purpose flour

3 tablespoons unsalted butter, chilled and cubed

3 tablespoons sugar

rhubarb custard

12 oz. rhubarb, trimmed and chopped into small pieces

⅔ cup sugar

3 eggs

a few drops of vanilla extract

½ cup heavy cream

a baking sheet, greased

6 x 3½-inch loose-based fluted tartlet pans, greased

makes 6

Creamy rhubarb custard tarts with crumbly butter biscuit on top. If you like, you can skip the crumble step and simply crush 6 oz. good, store-bought shortbread cookies instead. For an extra helping of decadence, serve with custard. If you have plenty of rhubarb, you can even make more of the mashed rhubarb, then push it through a sieve to make a lovely coulis for pouring onto the tartlet. Using forced rhubarb will make it a fantastic vibrant pink.

Preheat the oven to 350°F.

To make the crumble, mix the flour, butter, and sugar in a food processor. Bring the dough together with your hands and transfer to a lightly floured work surface. Roll with a rolling pin until about ⅛ inch thick, then place on the prepared baking sheet. Bake in the preheated oven for 15 minutes, or until pale gold. Remove from the oven (leaving the oven on) and leave to cool completely, then crush into crumbs and set aside.

To make the pastry dough, put the flour, butter, and sugar in a mixer until you get crumbs. Add the egg and mix again. Take the dough out of the mixer and bring together into a ball. If you prefer, you can make the dough by hand, but it's easier to do this if the butter is grated or very finely chopped.

Put the dough on a lightly floured work surface and roll with a rolling pin until ⅛ inch thick. Line the tartlet pans with the pastry and trim the excess neatly around the edges. Blind bake for 10 minutes, or until pale gold. Leave the oven on.

To make the rhubarb custard, put the rhubarb in a roasting pan, sprinkle over the sugar, and give it a stir. Cover with foil and roast in the hot oven for about 20–25 minutes, until soft. Remove from the oven, leave to cool for a few minutes, then blitz roughly in a food processor or mash with a fork.

Reduce the oven temperature to 300°F.

Whisk the eggs and vanilla extract together. Pour the cream into a saucepan over low heat and gently bring to a boil, stirring frequently. Remove from the heat and whisk in the eggs and vanilla and then the rhubarb until well combined.

Fill each tartlet crust up to the top with rhubarb custard and bake in the hot oven for 15–20 minutes, until the filling no longer wobbles when you shake the tartlet. Remove from the oven and scatter crumble over the top. Leave to cool slightly before serving or even better, serve chilled.

index

conversion charts

Weights and measures have been rounded up or down slightly to make measuring easier.

Volume equivalents:

American	Metric	Imperial
1 teaspoon	5 ml	
1 tablespoon	15 ml	
¼ cup	60 ml	2 fl.oz.
⅓ cup	75 ml	2½ fl.oz.
½ cup	125 ml	4 fl.oz.
⅔ cup	150 ml	5 fl.oz. (¼ pint)
¾ cup	175 ml	6 fl.oz.
1 cup	250 ml	8 fl.oz.

1 stick butter = 8 tablespoons = 125 g

Weight equivalents:

Imperial	Metric
1 oz.	25 g
2 oz.	50 g
3 oz.	75 g
4 oz.	125 g
5 oz.	150 g
6 oz.	175 g
7 oz.	200 g
8 oz. (½ lb.)	250 g
9 oz.	275 g
10 oz.	300 g
11 oz.	325 g
12 oz.	375 g
13 oz.	400 g
14 oz.	425 g
15 oz.	475 g
16 oz. (1 lb.)	500 g
2 lb.	1 kg

Measurements:

Inches	cm
¼ inch	5 mm
½ inch	1 cm
¾ inch	1.5 cm
1 inch	2.5 cm
2 inches	5 cm
3 inches	7 cm
4 inches	10 cm
5 inches	12 cm
6 inches	15 cm
7 inches	18 cm
8 inches	20 cm
9 inches	23 cm
10 inches	25 cm
11 inches	28 cm
12 inches	30 cm

Oven temperatures:

110°C	(225°F)	Gas ¼
120°C	(250°F)	Gas ½
140°C	(275°F)	Gas 1
150°C	(300°F)	Gas 2
160°C	(325°F)	Gas 3
180°C	(350°F)	Gas 4
190°C	(375°F)	Gas 5
200°C	(400°F)	Gas 6
220°C	(425°F)	Gas 7
230°C	(450°F)	Gas 8
240°C	(475°F)	Gas 9

credits

Key: a=above, b=below, r=right,
l=left, c=centre, bg = background.

recipe credits

Ghillie Basan
Pages 18l, 31l, 55l, 59r, 63l,
66l, 79l, 86, 104l, 113r

Fiona Beckett
Pages 63r, 83l, 84l, 112, 147,
173l, 173r, 187r

Celia Brooks Brown
Pages 108l, 125br

Maxine Clark
Pages 15bl, 23br, 31r, 41r, 55r,
60l, 69, 73ar, 76l, 79r, 89bl,
108r, 125ar, 145, 155l, 160l,
160r, 179r, 180l

Ross Dobson
Pages 11r, 12r, 16, 21, 23ar,
24, 37l, 38r, 46l, 46r, 51ar, 64,
66r, 70r, 75l, 84r, 93l, 94r, 97l,
97r, 103l, 103r, 107l, 107r, 118l,
132l, 134, 139r, 144, 151l,
156r, 159r, 167l, 167r, 169,
174l, 179l, 183l, 183r, 184l,

Tonia George
Pages 15br, 20, 27l, 41l, 60r,
87r, 127r, 131r, 135r, 177al

Brian Glover
Pages 114l, 117r, 118r, 120,
121, 131l

Amanda Grant
Pages 15al, 51al, 73al, 73br,
87l, 127l, 177br

Annie Nichols
Page 12

Jane Noraika
Page 17l

Elsa Petersen-Schepelern
Page 143ar

Louise Pickford
Pages 38l, 42r, 73bl, 83r, 101br,
151r, 155r, 177ar

Isidora Popovic
Pages 28, 32l, 56, 123, 104r,
114r, 132l, 152r, 174r, 188

Sarah Randell
Pages 33, 146, 159l, 163, 164,
184r

Annie Rigg
Page 143bl

Jennie Shapter
Page 125bl

Fiona Smith
Pages 17r, 32r, 65l, 65r, 70l,
76r, 89al, 98r, 101al, 109

Sonia Stevenson
Pages 15ar, 23al, 37r, 143br

Linda Tubby
Pages 42l, 45l, 45r, 51bl, 89ar,
135l

Sunil Vijayakar
Pages 94l, 101bl, 113l

Fran Warde
Pages 125al, 177bl

Laura Washburn
Pages 11l, 18r, 23bl, 27r, 49l,
49r, 59l, 75r, 89br, 93r, 98l,
101ar, 117l, 122, 139l, 140,
141l, 141r, 143al, 148r, 180r,
187l

Lindy Wildsmith
Pages 51br, 148l, 152l, 156l,
168,

photography credits

Martin Brigdale
Pages 4, 6br, 10, 18, 19, 22al,
22bl, 30, 37, 41, 44, 45, 48ar,
48bl, 50bl, 54ar, 56b, 58, 62,
69, 78, 88ar, 88br, 93, 109,
116, 122l, 142br, 154, 163,
181, 186

Peter Cassidy
Pages front endpapers, 5bl, bcl
& br, 6bl, 15ar, 15bl, 23ar, 23bl,
24bg, 27l, 27bg, 28bg, 29, 32,
33bg, 42 both, 46bg, 49, 51ar,
51bl, 54al, 54br, 55, 56bg, 57,
60bg, 63, 66, 69bg, 73ar, 73bl,
76bg, 80, 82, 83l, 84, 86 both,
88bl, 89ar, 89bl, 98 both,
101ar, 101bl, 103, 104ar,
104bg, 105, 106al, 107, 108bg,
110, 112 a & b, 114-115 all,
119, 120, 121l&r, 122r, 123 all,
124ar, 125ar, 125bl, 127l, 130,
133, 134bg, 135bg, 136, 138,
140-141 all, 142bl, 143ar,
143bl, 144b, 145l, 145r, 146
both, 151l&r, 153, 155, 156r,
160l&r, 161, 169bg, 172, 173,
175, 176ar, 177ar, 177bl, 179,
187, 189

Nicki Dowey
Pages 16bg, 84bg

Tara Fisher
Pages 2, 6ar, 14al, 50al, 50br,
72al, 72br, 87l, 122bg, 124bl,
126, 148, 152, 156l, 168l,
176br

Jonathan Gregson
Pages 5ar, 135, 167bg, 173bg,
176al, 179bg, 183bg

Caroline Hughes
Pages 33al, 48al, 76, 94

Richard Jung
Pages back endpapers, 3, 5acl,
acr, & bcr, 8, 11r, 12bg, 13,
16al, 17bg, 20r, 21al&ar, 22ar,
25, 28, 31l, 36, 38, 39, 46a
both, 47, 48br, 50ar, 52, 59,
65bg, 68, 71, 74, 79, 90, 92,
95, 96, 97, 102, 106ar, bl, &br,
113r, 117, 118, 128, 132, 134,
139 both, 144a, 149 l & r 157,
159, 166, 167, 170, 174, 182,
183, 184l, 188, 192

Sandra Lane
Page 63bg

Lisa Linder
Pages 66bg, 142al, 155bg

William Lingwood
Pages 54bl, 75

James Merrell
Page 142ar

Diana Miller
Pages 16ar, 17a, 31r, 56a, 65,
70, 72ar, 77, 88al, 99, 100al

David Munns
Pages 100ar

Noel Murphy
Pages 14bl, 21bg, 22br, 60,
108

Peter Myers
Pages 12, 14ar, 14br

Steve Painter
Page 15al, 15br, 18bg, 23al,
23br, 51al, 51br, 73al, 73br,
89al, 89br, 101al, 101br, 125al,
125br, 143al, 143br, 177al,
177br, 190-191

© Steve Painter
Page 1

William Reavell
Pages 45bg, 120bg

Claire Richardson
Pages 24, 104al, 168r

William Shaw
Page 124br

Yuki Sugiura
Pages 20l, 26, 40, 61, 87r,
127r, 131

Debi Treloar
Pages 124al, 176bl

Pia Tryde
Page 184r

Simon Upton
Page 11l

Ian Wallace
Pages 43, 72bl, 100br

Kate Whitaker
Pages 3bg, 5bg, 7, 9, 11bg,
31bg, 32bg, 33ar, 35, 37bg,
38bg, 41bg, 49bg, 53, 59bg,
64 both, 67, 70bg, 75bg, 79bg,
81, 83bg, 85, 87bg, 91, 93bg,
94bg, 97bg, 100bl, 103bg,
107bg, 111, 112bg, 113bg,
113l, 117bg, 118bg, 121bg,
127bg, 129, 131bg, 132bg,
137, 144bg, 145bg, 147,
148bg, 149bg, 150, 151bg,
152bg, 156bg, 158, 159bg,
160bg, 162, 163bg, 164bg,
165, 168bg, 169l&r, 171,
174bg, 178, 180bg, 184bg,
185, 187bg

Polly Wreford
Pages 5al, 6al, 34, 83r, 164,
180

Francesca Yorke
Page 188bg